D0035303

THE
CLIMB
UP TO
HELL

ALSO BY JACK OLSEN

Hastened to the Grave: The Gypsy Murder Investigation
Salt of the Earth: One Family's Journey through the Violent American
    Landscape
The Misbegotten Son
Predator: Rape, Madness, and Injustice in Seattle
Doc: The Rape of the Town of Lovell
Son: A Psychopath and His Victims

THE CLIMB UP TO HELL

BY JACK OLSEN

St. Martin's Griffin ⚞ New York

THE CLIMB UP TO HELL. Copyright © 1962, 1998 by
John Edward Olsen. Introduction copyright © 1998
by Trevanian. All rights reserved. Printed in the
United States of America. No part of this book may
be used or reproduced in any manner whatsoever
without written permission except in the case of
brief quotations embodied in critical articles or
reviews. For information, address St. Martin's
Press, 175 Fifth Avenue, New York, N.Y. 10010.

Library of Congress Cataloging-in-Publication Data

Olsen, Jack.
    The climb up to hell / by Jack Olsen.
        p. cm.
    Originally published by New York : Harper &
Row, 1962.
    ISBN 0-312-19450-1
    1. Mountaineering—Switzerland—Eiger—
History. 2. Eiger (Switzerland)—Description and
travel. I. Title.
GV199.44.S92E546   1998
914.94'54—dc21   98-33794
                                             CIP

First published in the United States by Harper &
Row

First St. Martin's Griffin Edition: November 1998

10 9 8 7 6 5 4 3 2 1

For Eula and Trip Child

and my son,

Alan

AUTHOR'S NOTE

As a citybound journalist, I never had to justify myself by answering the silly question "Why do men climb mountains?" I had neither the courage nor the passion to climb anything higher than a jungle gym, and I'd already heard the answer from many great alpinists, including my friend Lionel Terray, whom I first met in the Alps while gathering material for *The Climb Up to Hell.* In one of his many sensitive and perceptive works, Terray wrote:

> It is not the goal of grand alpinism to face peril, but it is one of the tests one must undergo to deserve the joy of rising for an instant above the state of crawling grubs.

Spectators peering almost straight up from the valley below Switzerland's Eiger mountain will spot no crawling grubs—a few fools, perhaps, but even the most ill-prepared flyspecks on the mile-high wall seem redeemed by their own antic bravado as they attack the murderous, rotting rock piton by piton and inch by inch, ducking (and not always in time) the rocks and boulders that cascade down the face like shrapnel. Sometimes these daredevils have to be saved by men like Terray, brave and resourceful rescuers driven by a sense of honor and empathy to protect the foolish from their folly. Huddled together in midnight darkness on the knife-edge ridge of the most dangerous ice-wall in the Alps, Lionel and his forty-nine colleagues carried out what many still consider the greatest rescue in Alpine history.

The 1957 events on the "Eiger Nordwand" continue to live in various incarnations. *The Climb Up to Hell* has been republished in Great Britain, in Italy (*Arrampicarsi All'Inferno*), France (*Quatre Hommes sur l'Eiger*), Hungary (*A Szörny*), and elsewhere. The novelist Trevanian revisited the dramatic setting in his bestseller *The Eiger Sanction*, later made into a movie starring Clint Eastwood. Arthur J. Roth told parts of the story in his 1982 book, *Eiger, Wall of Death*, and the Everest climber Jon Krakauer authored the recent *Eiger Dreams: Ventures Among Men and Mountains*. Even an opera on the great rescue is being composed in England.

"Why did you take the risk?" I asked "the good angel of Annapurna" on one of his visits to New York. "You didn't know these climbers. They weren't even French."

Lionel Terray replied, "*Ils étaient des hommes.* They were men."

In one of the terrible ironies with which alpinism abounds, my new friend flew back home to Chamonix and fell to his death on the Mont Blanc, the backyard and *terra cognita* of his own climbing career.

I dedicate this latest edition of *The Climb Up to Hell* to Lionel and his international band of brothers—German, French, Austrian, Swiss, Italian, Polish, Dutch—who risked death to save an unknown comrade on the north wall of the "Ogre," to the brave climbers who died then and later, and to Claudio Corti, the bold and foolhardy truck driver whose life hung from a whining wisp of cable six thousand feet above the valley floor and who lives today to tell his bravura tale in his hometown of Lecco, the shrine of Italian alpinism. *Ils étaient des hommes.*

Jack Olsen
Bainbridge Island, Washington
October 1998

INTRODUCTION

In the Iron Age of mountaineering, before a new generation of athlete/technicians began attacking mountains with space-age equipment and devices that they used as aids in ascending, rather than limiting their hardware to protection and rescue, as the sixth degree climbers of the old school did, every climb of the north face of the Eiger had its own tale of adventure, courage, and hardship. But none was more tragic, more heroic, and more bizarre than the ill-starred assault made in 1957 by as unprepared and unbalanced a four-man rope as one can imagine. The tragedy lay in the fact that three members of the rope died. Much of the heroism was shown by the mixed party of amateur rescuers from six nations who saved the survivor, while—typically, I'm afraid—the professional Swiss guides dallied and dithered and worried about who was going to pay them. What was bizarre about the climb was that four years were to pass before the climbing world learned that the assault had been successful . . . the thirteenth successful climb, and the alpine journals were not slow to underline this fateful number to their almost universally superstitious readers.

Beginning with a crisply written summary of early assaults on the north wall of the Eiger as a background to the tragic 1957 climb, Jack Olsen blends his long experience as a sports journalist with his skills as a bestselling novelist to lend technical accuracy to fascinating characterizations and a taut narrative structure that includes "counter-cutting" between the desperate fight for life on the face, the Herculean efforts of the rescuers, and the Greek chorus of the journalists and "death-tourists" watching from the comfortable hotels in the alpine valley below.

I was delighted to learn that Jack Olsen's *Climb Up to Hell* was going to be reissued, allowing a new generation of readers to thrill to one of the best accounts of true, high-mountain adventure ever written.

Trevanian,
author of *The Eiger Sanction*

part one
THE LIVING

CHAPTER ONE

Fritz von Almen, thirty-nine years old, serious of mien, conservative of dress, walked onto a tiny side porch of his family's hotel, 6,700 feet up in the Swiss Alps, and sat in front of a swivel-mounted pair of binoculars aimed at a towering mountain wall across the meadows. It was late on Sunday morning, August 4, 1957, and for the second day in a row, the weather favored von Almen's hobby of Alp-watching. The midsummer sun beat down and encouraged him; he knew that hot days made the chamois wander over to the base of the cliff to bask in the cooler stream of air pouring continually downward: nature's air conditioning. Von Almen felt optimistic as he swept the twin-barreled seventy-two-power Zeiss telescope across the rock litter at the base of the wall, then slowly worked his field of vision upward across gulch and crevasse, pillar and snow field. A few hundred yards up, silhouetted against a patch of dirtying snow, three fine chamois popped into sight. Von Almen watched the nimble miniature antelopes for a few minutes, savoring that quiet satisfaction that comes also to bird watchers and eclipse observers. Now, pleased by this good omen for the day, he stepped back into the hotel and to the daily humdrum of running it, as one member of his family or another had been doing for 117 years.

It is a frequently observed phenomenon of happenstance that awful catastrophes often take place in the most breathtaking of settings. In the gentle valleys of Grindelwald and Lauterbrunnen below Fritz von Almen's hotel, grassy slopes

3

of a rich green hue sweep upward, dotted with daisies, buttercups, clover and fat dandelions until they reach the first patches of snow above, where white crocuses, snowbells and violets make their appearance. The trees, from valley floor to timberline, run the whole spectrum of greens from near-black through lime to a brilliant chartreuse that shows as bright splashes in the dark stands of conifers. Everywhere wisps of waterfalls soar over the cliffs into the valley. Some of them disappear into the air on the long drop toward the floor or plume off into nothingness on the high winds which sweep up the canyons. Some of the waterfalls drop inside the mountains, break out into space again farther down, then fall back inside, there to work their way through the earth before appearing for the last time as little rivulets in the valley. All of them end up in two streams: the Black Lütschine and the White Lütschine, which finally join to make a small river. Milky with glacier dust, the river performs the endless task of carrying away the bits and pieces slowly being ground off the high mountains by glacier, wind and water.

Here in the Bernese Oberland, heartland of the Swiss Alps, the hand of man is unobtrusive. A few small scallops of level land, tilled with fierce determination by dogged farmers, have been sliced from the hilltops. Cogwheel railways begin in the valley and wind up past the ski-resort hotels like von Almen's and go almost to the top of the Oberland's highest mountain, the Jungfrau. With polished steel drive shafts pumping furiously, the little trains hum and whine and clack as they move upward past flashing mountain brooks, picture-book chalets and shepherds' huts perched on the hillsides, until they pierce through the very insides of the mountains in tunnels which run for miles.

Going up, one soon passes through the first ranges of brown cliffs and mountains, sheer and crumbling. Just before the timberline there are clumps of miniature firs, a few inches tall but fully developed, like dwarf Japanese master-pieces. Ledges of shale and slate, edging their way inexorably toward the valley floor, lie in pinnate patterns like giant ferns. Then one sees the tall, final conifers, the patches of dirty rock-soiled snow, and finally the region of eternal snow. Here only the hardy plants like saxifrage, Veronica and rock speedwell can exist, but animals abound. Prime object of Alp-watchers like von Almen is the ibex, a sort of wild mountain sheep, protected from hunters by a five-hundred-dollar penalty, and admired for its graceful feats of mountaineering. The smaller chamois romp about, defying all of Newton's Laws, in a constant hunt for the *pièce de résistance* of their existence: the Thlaspi *rotundifolium,* a cress-like plant with pale lilac flowers. Alpine weasels, wearing drab brown coats in summer and ermine in winter, hug the ice on the ridges, and stone martens clamber all over the highest peaks; climbers have tracked them up one side of the Jungfrau and down the other. Overhead fly wondrous birds: Alpine crows possessed of such flying skill that they seek out storms and play on the shock waves of the wind; they are equaled only by swallows in their aerobatic ability. Magpies fling themselves twenty feet straight up, then hover in one spot, singing all the time, and suddenly let themselves plane down, singing until they touch the ground and turn off their arias. In the Bernese Oberland, it is said that spring sometimes comes early just to hear the magpies. Even on the uppermost peaks, where no life is visible to the naked eye, Alpine birds inspect the fissures and faces for spiders and bugs. Nature equipped these birds with crampons: little hooks and points on their claws, enabling them to climb like flies. They are the envy of mountaineers.

Halfway up on the long hauls from the valley floors to the highest points on the cogwheel railroads, the trains suddenly burst above the foothills and cliffs which until then have blocked the travelers' view, and the dominant characteristic of the Bernese Oberland comes into awesome sight. Glazed with ice and mantled in perpetual snow, some of the most famous mountains of Europe leap into blue-white focus. The Wetterhorn, the Blümlisalp, the Bietschhorn, the Schreckhorn, the Finsteraarhorn poke upward in apparent immutability. But most conspicuous of all is a mighty trinity of peaks lying side by side on the vast bulk of the Jungfrau Massif. Jutting upward from the broad base of the Massif are the Eiger (13,038 feet), the Mönch (13,465 feet) and the Jungfrau peak itself (tallest at 13,638 feet), juxtaposed like this:

JUNGFRAU MASSIF

The smallest is the killer. The great German climber Andreas Heckmeier called the Eiger "the last great problem in the Alps." Centuries before, the Interlaken monks, without ever setting foot on the mountain, had known instinctively that it was an evil place. The two higher mountains of the triumvirate were given benign names: Mönch (monk) and Jungfrau (virgin). But to the jutting pyramid lying alongside, the monks affixed the word for ogre, and history has borne out the aptness of their choice. Two of the faces of the Eiger present difficult but traditional climbing problems; the third face is a 6,000-foot concave wall facing north, a tilted saucer of rotten rock, waterfalls, hanging ice fields and gullies scoured smooth by thousands of years of avalanche. Even its geology is different from the other mountains of the Oberland. The Eiger, the highest limestone mountain in Europe and the eyetooth of the Oberland, is a geological accident. Upheavals of undersea ranges forced it into being. A massive "flake" from another range was deposited on it, and then the whole was kneaded and twisted and tumbled about through millions of years until the Eiger was formed into a crazy quilt of hectic stratification, helter-skelter crystalline splotches and a thin coating of softer limestone which covered the whole mountain like a disintegrating rind. All the storms of northern Europe break across the perpendicular mass of the Eiger north wall, and it is on this wall that the forces of weathering have produced the ultimate in mountain-climbing challenges. The lower half of the cliff has been rubbed almost clean of the soft, rotten limestone covering, and the result is pitch after pitch of smooth, holdless rock, usually glazed with ice. But the upper half still bulges with the porous facing which is slowly being pried loose by wind and rains and tumbled down the cliff. The result is a "living" mountain, forever seething and pulsating and changing, frigidly volatile and willy-nilly murderous. One risks death from falling stones to stand at its base and look up at a mile of cliff and crevasse, ice field and waterfall, lying in almost total shadow. There is no mountain or cliff in the world so fraught with what climbers call "objective" dangers—perils like avalanche and rockfall and blizzard over which the climber, regardless of his skill, has no control. In warm weather, the "mountain artillery" cascades in ear-splitting salvos and barrages, then skips off to fall unimpeded for thousands of feet to the base. Tons of snow from the summit hiss down in deadly, smothering avalanche. Electrically charged clouds swirl into the wall, enshrouding climbers, flicking sparks from their pitons, wreathing their heads in St. Elmo's fire, while the whole face hums and whines like a monster power generator. Night bivouacs become fights for survival. Often the climber must sleep in a sitting position, legs dangling over the wall, with ropes fixed to the unstable rock as the only protection against a fall. At worst, one must stand on a thin ledge all night, flattened against the mountain, enduring high winds, whipping snow and sub-zero temperatures. And the next morning one must somehow summon the strength to begin again the wracking attack on the special problems of the north wall: three slick ice fields; long traverses (sideway movements) across polished, sheer cliffs offering no handholds and hardly any cracks in which to drive a piton; a hanging ice field which collects and redistributes all the avalanches of the upper level; narrow rock chimneys up which the climber, heavy-laden with gear, must inch himself; drenching falls of super-cooled water; and finally a summit snow field pitched at an easier fifty-degree angle but with a tendency toward massive snowslides which have swept climbers to their deaths when victory was only yards away.

For centuries, no one climbed mountains, reckoning it a crazy man's pursuit. But even when climbing became popular, and adventure-seeking English schoolteachers and desk-bound German clerks were scrambling all over the Alps, the Eiger north wall remained untouched. Those who thought about it—and there were many expert climbers among them—took one look and said, "Impossible." The Zürich newspaper, Sport, wrote as late as the mid-1930's:

> The ascent of the Eiger north wall is forbidden. It is not the administration in Bern which has pronounced the veto. It is the Eiger itself speaking with mute language no one can fail to understand. If someone fails to comprehend the message, he must be deaf, and deserves to be hauled away from the danger area exactly as one would lead a blind man off the streetcar tracks to the pavement.

Hardly had these words been written when a rope of Germans confirmed *Sport's* hypothesis. They had barely begun to work their way up the face when they fell and hung helplessly from their ropes, anchored by pitons and snap links. Luckily for those foolhardy trail breakers, there was a gallery opening on the face of the Eiger. When the cogwheel train tunnel was being hacked through the innards of the mountain, this hole had been used as a dumping hatch for rock. The tunnel completed, the hole was covered over by heavily bolted doors. Through the years this aperture was to play a major role in rescues and rescue attempts. The German rope became the first thus to be saved by brave Swiss guides who pulled them into the railroad tunnel to safety. Angered by the attempt and the useless risking of lives, the Swiss launched long tirades against the German climbers. For answer, two bold climbers from Munich set up shop in a cow hut in the meadows of Alpiglen, just below the face, and began to study the possible routes for an ascent. They were Max Sedlmayer and Karl Mehringer, skilled climbers, painstakingly careful practitioners of their craft, representatives of the elite of German mountaineers.

At two in the morning of August 21, 1935, Sedlmayer and Mehringer began their attack on the mountain, over the so-called "most direct" route, up the middle of the face to the summit. As day broke, Alp-watchers at the von Almens' little complex of hotels in Kleine Scheidegg spotted the climbers in their telescopes, and observed that they were proceeding in good style. By dark on that first day, the two Germans had reached a point 2,600 feet up the cliff after solving a long series of smooth malm steps. The next day they faced a vertical pitch of three hundred feet on polished rock. As they groped upward, the mountain artillery went to work, and watchers below could see them time and again covering their heads with their rucksacks and their hands as the killing rockfalls whistled by them. That same day they covered the vast first ice field, but now they were beginning to show signs of fatigue. On the third day of their climb, they made slow and tedious progress, halting every few minutes to cover up against falling rocks. That night the weather changed without warning—a commonplace on the Eiger north wall—and the climbers disappeared from sight in the storm. Not till noon on the fourth day of the assault did the clouds part to reveal the face. Miraculously, there were Sedlmayer and Mehringer moving slowly across another ice field. But now it was plain—to experienced mountaineers, if not to the tourists gawking through the telescopes—that they were too exhausted to make the top, or, for that matter, to clamber back down the smooth cliffs now glazed with clear ice. Another storm hit that night, and all signs of human activity stopped on the precipice. Weeks later, Ernst Udet, Germany's World War I ace, flew across the face of the Eiger to see if he could spot the bodies of his countrymen. Flying dangerously close, buffeted about by tricky air currents, the famous German flier made out the pattern of a body frozen to the wall in an upright position. The two climbers had died in a stand-up bivouac. Thus ended all attempts on the north wall in 1935.

But there was a sort of Wagnerian madness in Germany in those years; young men happily subjected themselves to extreme tests for the glory of the Fatherland, and the bodies of Sedlmayer and Mehringer, still pinned in death to the ice of the wall, only served as a stimulus for more upward suicides. First to arrive at the Eiger in 1936 were two more men from Munich—Albert Herbst and Hans Teufel. It was May, and a single look convinced them that it was too early in the season to attempt to climb the face or recover the bodies of their two townsmen. They decided to make some training climbs on the nearby Schneehorn, an ice-and-snow-covered mountain which is far less demanding than the Eiger. They reached the summit, but on the way back an avalanche carried them down six hundred feet. Teufel broke his neck against a rock ledge; Herbst was saved. It was an ominous start, but no deterrent to certain other wild-eyed young Teutons. Before a week had gone by, two Austrians, Edi Rainer and Willy Angerer, pitched a tent in the meadows near the Kleine Scheidegg hotels to seek out a new route to the top of the north wall. Soon they were joined by two German soldiers, Toni Kurz and Andreas Hinterstoisser, members of an elite mountain-ranger unit, and early on the morning of July 18 the four bold climbers began their assault. They did, indeed, open up a new route on the face, one which later was to be used by successful climbing parties. By skillful use of the rope and pitons, Hinterstoisser moved 130 feet across a seemingly impossible slanting traverse which ultimately proved to be the key to the entire ascent. Once on the other side, he fixed his rope securely to another piton, and the remaining three climbers came across the lifeline. But an awful mistake was made. The traversing rope, firmly in position, was retrieved.

Watched from the Kleine Scheidegg telescopes, the climbers now appeared inspired and strong. One by one, they vanquished difficult pitches, cramponed across the first ice field, and reached the "Red Cliff" leading to the second ice field. But suddenly the two Austrians, Rainer and Angerer, were seen to stop. Kurz and Hinterstoisser, up above on a narrow ledge, lowered a rope and pulled the pair alongside. The climbers, now linked as a rope of four, were already halfway up the wall, a remarkable climb on a single day. But Angerer plainly was in trouble, barely able to negotiate on the slippery rock. The next day, the party again moved upward, but far more slowly, with frequent stops to nurse Angerer, who seemed to have a head wound. On the following morning they gave up and headed down. With precise movements they lowered themselves on the doubled rope, and as night fell they had crossed the first ice field. Now they had only to reverse the traverse pioneered by Hinterstoisser, rope down the "Difficult Crack," and the rest would be relatively simple. On July 21, their fourth day on the mountain, they reached Hinterstoisser's traverse and found that the Eiger north wall, in its usual quixotic fashion, had changed. The temperature had dropped sharply. The water which had been cascading down the face now had frozen against the sheer walls of the traverse. All day long the brave and skillful Hinterstoisser could be seen attacking the polished ice of the cliff, and all day long he was beaten back. Finally, the four climbers were seen trying to lower themselves straight down the sheer cliff, 650 feet deep, to the easier pitches below. As the afternoon mists deepened, a sector guard on the railway opened the heavy doors and shouted across the wall on the slim chance that one of the climbers would answer him. To his amazement, he could hear the yodels of the four men. One of them shouted:

"We're coming down. All's well!" The guard went inside to brew them some tea.

Two hours later no visitors had arrived. The guard opened the doors again and called into the mists. But now there were no happy yodels or cheers of optimism. The voice of Toni Kurz called weakly: "Help! Help! The others are all dead. I am the only one alive. Help!"

The guard ran to the telephone and called down to the mountainside town of Wengen for rescuers. Up the railroad on a special train came three crack guides: Hans Schlunegger and the brothers Rubi: Christian and Adolf. They stepped onto the face through the gallery doors and began a slow, dangerous traverse which brought them three hundred feet below the point where Kurz was hanging in a rope sling. They could go no farther on the slick ice, and night was coming on. They called to Kurz. What had happened? "Hinterstoisser came off and fell the whole way down," Kurz answered. "The rope pulled Rainer up against a snap link. He froze to death there. And Angerer's dead, too, hanging below me, strangled by the rope when he fell."

Now the guides had to tell Kurz that they could go no farther on the icy precipice. "You can't rescue me from below!" the anguished German shouted. But the Swiss guides knew that they would be hard pressed even to get back to the safety of the gallery window. They told Kurz he would have to stick it out, alone and exposed, for another night. "No!" he screamed. "No! No!" Making their retreat, the guides could hear Kurz's shouts all the way, alternately pleading and vilifying and arguing that he could not endure in the sub-zero temperatures. But endure he did. His mittenless left hand froze into a useless blob. The water thawed by his body ran down to the tips of his crampons, where it formed long icicles on the spikes. But he was still alive when the guides, in the light of dawn, beat their way back across the mountain to a point 130 feet below his perch. Now they reached a vertical pitch, bulging outward and covered with ice, which even unglazed would have taxed the skills of the best cliff climbers. There they halted and shouted to Kurz, out of sight behind the bulge above them. "Can you get a rope down?" they asked. "Then we could attach all the gear you need."

Kurz answered that he had no line. Christian Rubi hit on a macabre plan. He told Kurz to climb down to Angerer and cut the rope fixing Angerer's body to the wall. By untwisting the frozen strands, he might salvage enough line to lower to his rescuers. This simple maneuver took the half-dead Kurz, working with one good hand, his ice ax and his teeth, six hours. But from it he gained enough rope to lower to the rescue team. They fastened to it two lengths of rope, joined by a thick knot, and pitons, snap links and a hammer, everything Kurz would require to rope himself down the pitch. Up went the rescue gear, and for an hour Kurz busied himself with the tedious task of driving a piton one-handedly into the wall and fixing the new rope to it. Then he connected his sling to the rope with a snap link and began inching his way downward. Below, the guides shouted encouragement and waited, and after a long vigil they saw the soles of Kurz's boots scrape into sight above them, hang there, and stop. The snap link which fixed him to his lifeline had come up against the knot joining the two ropes and jammed tight. His feet dangling just a few feet above the rescuers' reach, Toni Kurz fumbled with the ice-encrusted knot for a short time, muttered, "I'm finished," slumped forward and died.

Twelve more men have died on the north wall in the succeeding years, making eighteen in all; others have retreated with broken limbs, mashed hands, bleeding heads and severe frostbite; and sixteen parties, the first an Austro-German rope in 1938, have successfully climbed the wall. And still the long-ago death of Toni Kurz is recalled with vivid memory by the mountain folk, perhaps because this was one of the last few times that their own Swiss guides would risk their lives in rescue attempts on the face, perhaps because of the dramatic few feet of difference between death and rescue, perhaps because of young Kurz's brave fight for life. "He had hung in his rope-sling buffeted by the storm, but determined not to surrender," wrote Sir Arnold Lunn. "And he did not surrender. He died. In the annals of mountaineering there is no record of a more heroic endurance."

CHAPTER TWO

But for all their deep personal respect for the courage of Toni Kurz, the Bernese did not want a repetition of such bravado. Partly this was simple self-preservation: men who climbed the Eiger risked not only their own lives but those of the Swiss guides who had to go up after them. Here the Oberlanders had logic on their side. But there was another side to it, this one less reasonable. Much of the resentment against the elite climbers came from a deeply inbred dislike, distrust and distaste for foreigners, even those "foreigners" who came from a few miles away. One had to see it from the Bernese point of view. For hundreds of years, residents of this isolated district of glacier and mountain had hacked and scraped their very existences out of infinitesimally small plots of valley land, had grazed their goats and cows high up on the side of barely arable mountains, had protected themselves against avalanche and storm with the most primitive means. Switzerland was isolated by its mountains from Europe, but the Bernese Oberland was isolated even from the rest of Switzerland. Schweizerdeutsch, the variant of German spoken throughout most of Switzerland, is itself a product of isolation. But the Oberlanders did not even speak a standard Schweizerdeutsch. Years of living in tiny villages, with only the barest contact with the next village and no contact whatever beyond that, produced a sort of decelerating speech, a slowed-down speech to match their slowed-down, tortuous mode of life. The Bernese Oberlanders were trapped in their mountains. No mistakes could be tolerated in dealing with the awful forces of nature surrounding them, and nothing could be wasted. There was a saying: "If a man from the Bernese Oberland eats a nail, a screw will come out." Such a way of life, spread over a couple of centuries, had produced a possessive, isolationist, xenophobic people, incapable of seeing anything in terms reaching beyond the nearest mountain range. Every thought, every concept, had to be recast to fit *their* valley and *their* river and *their* mountain. An aristocrat of the Lauterbrunnen Valley summed up the attitude in a recounting of an apocryphal conversation between a visiting American and a farmer from the Bernese Oberland:

SWISS FARMER: It takes me one whole hour to walk around my farm.

AMERICAN: It takes me half a day to drive around mine.

SWISS FARMER: Yes, I used to have a bad car like that.

What the Oberlander *could* comprehend and embrace was his independence, the *raison d'être* of the whole Helvetian State, but most particularly embraced in the Bernese Oberland. "We have the most freedom in the world," the Oberlanders said proudly. "We have even the freedom not to be free, if we choose." Cantonal and federal authorities had the devil's own time establishing any enforceable laws in the Oberland, not because the people were anything but law-abiding, but simply because they regarded every law, every regulation, every rule as an attack on their independence. There used to be no speed limit in the Oberland, and maniacal vacationers from the rest of Europe would imperil the lives of the natives each time they barreled into a village at high speed. Yet it took the authorities years to establish local speed laws to protect the residents. Hardly any villagers owned cars, or ever would, but if the day came when they did own one, they wanted the freedom to drive it as fast as they could. Slow-moving vehicles like goat carts and bicycles were required by Swiss law to bear red reflectors, to protect the natives from nighttime drivers speeding on blind turns and steep hills. In the Bernese Oberland, these inexpensive safety devices were hardly to be seen. The Oberlander clung to his walking, strolling, carting independence. Let the driver beware; the locals figured they were already protected enough by a Swiss law holding the driver of a vehicle responsible for all accidents involving pedestrians, no matter what their cause. Thus one found the proud peasants walking down the main lane of a highway, ignoring all horns, and grandly signaling the driver to steer around them. This was Bernese independence, an arrogant, stubborn, truculent independence which seemed to say to the visitor, "This is my valley, this is my road, this is my countryside, these are my mountains. I have had to work hard for them, and my ancestors before me, and you do not belong here."

This was the attitude faced by climbers from Germany, Austria, Italy, France and Britain as they infiltrated the Oberland to carry out their ritualistic jousts with death. And there was, on top of all that, a special resentment of the Eiger climbers that went even beyond the usual dislike of *Ausländers*. Explained Kaspar von Almen of the hotel-keeping von Almens:

"Our people are deeply religious, and it has always seemed to them that cliff climbers should not be allowed to risk the life God has given them. They felt that whatever may be gained was far out of proportion to the dangers involved. And they felt that most of the men who attacked the north wall were show-offs. The north wall is the classical Alpine theater, a vertical stage open to anyone with normal eyesight and a pocket telescope. It has attracted many brave men, many world-ranking climbers. But it also has attracted far more than its share of show-offs, publicity seekers and just plain psychopaths."

Even before the grisly deaths of the Kurz team, the local

resentment of north wall climbers had spawned a declaration by the chief guide of Grindelwald, one of the two valley towns where Eiger parties can catch the cogwheel upward to the base of the cliff. He wrote:

> One cannot help regarding the contemplated climbing attempts on the north wall of the Eiger with serious misgivings. They are a plain indication of the great change which has taken place in the conception of the sport of mountaineering. We must assume that visitors who take part in such attempts are aware of the dangers they themselves are risking. But no one can expect the dispatch of guides, in unfavorable conditions, on a rescue operation in case of any further accidents on the Eiger's north wall. . . . We should find it impossible to force our guides to take a compulsory part in the kind of acrobatics which others are undertaking voluntarily.

After the deaths of Sedlmayer, Mehringer, Kurz and the others, local resentment of assaults on the Eiger reached a peak, and matters were only aggravated by some preclimb remarks of Angerer and Rainer, widely quoted after their deaths. Full of the foolhardiness of youth and the cocksureness of men who know their way around the mountains, the two young Austrians had told anyone who would listen that they were going to climb the north wall for one reason: "Because it has to be climbed, and you Swiss won't do it!" The Oberland mentality could not tolerate such remarks, however jokingly they were intended, and the guides of the valleys below the Eiger were urged to put an end to all rescues on the face. Early in July, 1937, a pronunciamento went out from the government in Bern:

> Parties intending to climb the north wall must be duly warned by the rescue stations and by the guides before they start on the ascent. In particular their

attention must be drawn to the fact that, in the event of an accident, no rescue operations will be undertaken.

Samuel Brawand, former guide, first to climb the Mittellegi ridge of the Eiger, and later a lecturer and member of the Swiss National Council, addressed himself to the matter in an interview in the *Neue Zürcher Zeitung.* "If people up there shout for help and the guides are in a position to bring them that help," he said, "then of course they will always do so. The only time they won't do it is when the dangers are so great as to make it obvious that no rescue attempt could stand a possible chance of success." Brawand noted that the administration in Bern once had banned all climbing on the north wall, then had quickly withdrawn the ban. "Rightly so," he said. ". . . You cannot really put a veto on any given method of committing suicide." In an oblique appeal to the young hotbloods who even then were making camp at the base of the mountain for still more assaults, Brawand added: "It should be remembered that there are more important tasks in this world than the ascent of the Eiger's north wall. I have myself taken part in first ascents and know how uncommonly satisfying such successes are; but one knows, too, that they are only steps in human development."

Sport of Zürich asked:

> Is it either good or necessary that this realm of nature's tremendous forces be invaded by beings which were not created as carefree mountain eagles or climbing plants, but as humans? The urge to achieve cannot be used as an excuse for self-annihilation. It is easy enough to call this a sporting activity, but sport does not necessarily mean the ultimate in achievement. To clear one's mind, it is only necessary to recall the *mens sana in corpore sano* of the ancients.

But the men pitching their tents in the meadows below the face were not philosophers. They were young, tough climbers, exponents of a fast-developing new school of mountaineers who scorned the classic, traditional climbs and sought instead awful cliffs and towers like the west face of the Dru, the Walker Spur in the Grandes Jorasses, the north face of the Western Zinne, the Civetta Wall, Piz Badile and the Eiger north wall. If there was an easy route to a summit, they scorned it. If there was a dangerous, difficult way, they climbed it, returned to the valley, and then sought out a still more dangerous way up. On their backs clanked rucksacks full of metallic items: rock-pitons which were driven into cracks until they gave off a clear musical note; longer ice-pitons with sharp barbs; twelve-pointed crampons for walking on ice; snap links which were hooked onto pitons and which made possible all sorts of rope tricks; ice daggers and ice axes and hammers. This was the beginning of the so-called Iron Age of mountaineering, and it was not without its detractors. There was a classical school of climbing purism which held that mountains should be climbed "organically," by logical and natural routes carefully and reasonably sought out. The classicists were just as courageous and skillful as any of the aerial acrobats of the ironmongery school, but they held it to be the height of folly, and a perversion of the true spirit of mountaineering, to attack mountains and cliffs abounding in objective dangers like avalanche and rockfall. They felt that climbing such mountains was like taking part in a crap game with one's life as the stakes. And they deplored the overuse of artificial devices like snap links, pitons and rope ladders.

These classicists counted as one of their heroes Dr. Hans Lauper, who had climbed the northeast wall of the Eiger in 1932. This climb, a masterpiece of planning and finesse, was over the "organic" route; it required vast reserves of climbing skill and strength; yet it avoided objective dangers. But the Iron Age mountaineers, reading about Lauper's conquest in the newspapers, felt that it lacked the razzle-dazzle of a climb straight up the north face. Their attitude led Dr. Günther Langes, a purist, to comment: "The so-called 'opening up' [of new routes] has reached dimensions which are, for the most part, pointless, because they were not done in order to win new and desirable routes from the mountains, but merely to mark a last free strip, somewhere in the rock, with a new route, and so record one's name as having achieved a first. But who is to count the number of variants which are no more than an error in a route that organically has been correctly carried out?"

Col. E. L. Strutt, another purist and editor of *The Alpine Journal,* said: "The Eiger north wall, still unscaled, continues to be an obsession for the mentally deranged of almost every nation. He who first succeeds may rest assured that he has accomplished the most imbecile variant since mountaineering first began."

Students of world history will not be surprised that in the context of the mid-1930's, it was the Germans and Austrians who took the lead in searching out the "imbecile variant." With each new tragedy on the wall, more fair-haired "Aryans" arrived to fling themselves at the Eiger north wall in the upward attempt at self-destruction. The Germans have a word for it—*Todeslieb*—and while it is folly to attribute special characteristics to races or nations, it was nonetheless obvious that in the years of the Nazi rise to power the Teutons seemed to have had almost a monopoly on the love of death, at least in the mountains. They all but bathed Nanga Parbat in blood, leaving twenty-seven dead on this 26,660-foot Asian mountain in two expeditions, and still returned for more. To the Austro-German deaths on the Eiger, they reacted almost with eagerness. "We have an irresistible urge to conquer the last, the most gigantic wall of the Alps," one of them wrote. "Let us plunge into the impossible and force our way through so long as there is breath left in our bodies. The death of so many good comrades must be atoned for at once!"

The great French climber, Lionel Terray, said: "I do not understand the German motivation for climbing. German climbers are very, very mad. It is something in the German soul, a mystic heroism."

In the popular novel *The White Tower,* by James Ramsey Ullman, a Swiss guide muses: "We Swiss—yes, and the English and French and Americans too—we climb mountains for sport. But the Germans, no. What it is they climb for I do not know. Only it is not for sport."

What most of the Germans were climbing for in the mid-1930's was, indeed, not sport. They climbed for the Fatherland. Ullman later wrote in *The Age of Mountaineering:* "Aflame with the hero-philosophy of Nazi-Fascism and egged on by flag-wavers and tub-thumpers at home, brown and blackshirted young climbers began vying with one another in what they conceived to be feats of courage and skill. All or nothing was their watchword—victory or death. No risk was too great, no foolhardiness to be condemned, so long as their exploits brought kudos to the *Vaterland.* . . ." Yet it is difficult, in the perspective of hindsight, to blame them. They were, after all, citizens of the Reich; they were not the formulators of state socialism or anti-Semitism; they were, for the most part, early victims of that tyranny and jingoism which later was to kill millions; they were not geopolitical, intellectual giants, but simple and brave men stimulated into action of a foolhardy nature and on behalf of a monstrously criminal cause.

It would have been all but impossible for a young German climber of that era to turn his attention away from the Eiger north wall. Each new death brought forth a spate of

propagandistic encouragement to other would-be con-
querors of the most treacherous face in the world. "A
climber has fallen," began one such blast. "Let a hundred
others rise for the morrow. . . . All our wars will always
take place in the mountains, and the cult of mountaineering
passionately pursued, and spreading more and more among
our young men, will contribute to the military preparedness
of the young generation." Hitler himself proclaimed that the
first men to climb the Eiger north wall would be awarded
gold medals at the Berlin Olympic games of 1936.

The Swiss sat back and watched and tried to understand.
A Swiss newspaper, viewing the awful deaths of the Toni
Kurz party with uncommon compassion, reported:

> Perhaps these young men have nothing more to
> lose. . . . What is to become of a generation to
> which society offers no social existence and which
> has only one thing left to look forward to: a single
> day's glory, the swiftly tarnishing highlight of a single
> hour? To be a bit of a hero, a bit of a soldier, sports-
> man or record-breaker, a gladiator, victorious one
> day, defeated the next. . . . The four recent vic-
> tims of the Eiger's north wall were pitiable crea-
> tures. . . .

No such compassion was shown, however, toward another class of climber: the Alpine phonies who attacked the
north wall purely for publicity and self-aggrandizement, or,
worse yet, came to the lower valleys loudly proclaiming
that they would climb the mountain but had, in reality, no
such intentions. They merely flitted from dinner party to
dinner party, loudly boasting of their plans and turning
away compliments with false modesty.

But also in the vanguard of potential wall climbers were
many men who were neither phonies, storm troopers nor

publicity hounds, but simply courageous mountaineers who did not agree that an attack on the Eiger north wall was in violation of classical climbing spirit. They felt it to be, instead, the supreme test of a climber's skill. It lured them and challenged them and intrigued them. They knew that they were obsessed irrationally, but, like the Austrian journalist Kurt Maix, they felt that climbing was "the most royal irrationality." They regarded an attempt on the north wall as the capstone of Alpine adventure. (Indeed, nearly twenty years later the French climber Maurice Herzog, on being told that the conquest of Annapurna had cost him his toes and his fingers, broke into tears and told another member of the expedition: "I'll never do the Eiger now, and I wanted to so much.") Many a calm, orderly man went quietly about the business of planning an attack on the mountain, ignoring charges of publicity-seeking and notoriety. They were reminiscent of Leslie Stephen, a classic climber who answered a similar charge by saying, "No more argument is possible than if I were to say that I liked eating olives, and someone asserted that I really eat them only out of affectation. My reply would be simply to go on eating olives."

And finally, in the broad spectrum of men who were lured by the Eiger north wall, there were the genuine neurotics, the compulsive, driven Ahab-like men who climbed not for Fatherland, not for the classic motives of adventure and challenge, not even for publicity or money or notoriety, but simply because they *had* to, because deep down in the wellsprings of their psychological being lurked defects of character and personal integration which forced them, with or without the necessary skills, to attack the wall. These men, in the last analysis, were the most dangerous to themselves, and to others.

On Monday morning, August 5, 1957, Fritz von Almen returned to his powerful telescope to search out the tracks of the three chamois he had spotted the day before. But instead of animal tracks, he saw deep steps hacked into the ice. Slowly, his hands trembling with excitement, he raised the heavy Zeiss binoculars. Near the Hinterstoisser traverse, he saw four climbers on the wall.

CHAPTER THREE

Death followed Claudio Corti like a faithful puppy dog. He came from the grimly drab village of Olginate, a seedy neighbor of the resort town of Lecco, near Lake Como, mecca for Italian Alpinists. Near Olginate and Lecco were the jutting needles and crags of the Crigna range, sawtoothed foothills of the Italian Alps; and those who lived in their shadows soon became inured to fatalities in the mountains. Every year a dozen or two Italian climbers fell to their deaths from the spurs and cornices of the Crigna, and still the attempts persisted. It was not that life was cheap to the northern Italians, or that they were in love with death, but simply that they had a touching, almost fatalistic belief in God, and very little else to do with themselves. They went up the spires and cliffs because climbing was "the only game in town," and they told themselves that God already had decided their fate, and so it did not matter whether they were home in bed or high on a sheer wall when their time arrived. They drove like the wind, and wheeled their babies on superhighways, for the same reason.

Like the young Germans flinging their bodies up into space for the Fatherland, the simple climbers of northern Italy were victims rather than villains. Corti's village of Olginate offered not even the picturesque flair and style of the tiny villages of Bavaria or the valley towns of Switzerland. It was merely dirty and dull. The five hundred villagers worked in factories making chains, lamps, nails, thread, wire and cartons. There was tenant farming on plots of land owned by the Roman Catholic church. The richest farmer in the village had one cow. To eke out an existence, most of the other villagers tilled small areas of land, forty or fifty feet square, kept a few rabbits, and went to their dreary jobs in the factories. Social life consisted of meeting in alleyways for conversation, or standing around the *trattoria* drinking beer and grappa and listening to the fancy sports cars of vacationing Germans whine by on the road to Lecco. It was a life which would have led many an otherwise normal man straight to the mountains, there, at least, to break the monotony.

But for Claudio Corti, going to the mountains was more than an escape; it was an obsession. Through most of his childhood, his father, a bricklayer, was away in Switzerland, working with the gangs of northern Italians sent out as cheap labor. For play, Claudio fished in the river winding down to Lake Como. But he soon tired of this and glanced upward. He was a powerful young man, carrying 154 sinewy, muscular pounds and standing five feet six and a half inches tall. He had the muscle development and oversized fingers and hands of a much larger man, and, from the beginning, mountaineering came easy to him. Time and again he used his tremendous strength to get out of fixes which would have finished another climber. Although he learned finesse, brute force was always his mainstay. By the time he was seventeen, he had made climbs of the "sixth degree"—the most difficult ascents possible by the Alpinists' system of grading—and had even established a few new routes (some would have called them "imbecile variants") up the minor mountains around Lecco. A frequent ropemate, Carlo Mauri of Lecco, member of many international expeditions, described his old friend with frankness:

"In Alpinism, as in any art, one can have a natural talent, and Claudio had this. But it is not enough to have the talent. One must study and prepare and polish one's talents to an even higher degree. This, Claudio never did. He was an instinctive climber, but he thought one merely had to *climb*, that strength was everything. He was physically capable of almost any climb, but not in the mind. And he did not climb from a natural love of Alpinism. To me, it always seemed that Claudio was a child on the mountains, a child possessed of great natural ability and tremendous strength, but nevertheless a child trying to show his father that he is not afraid."

Another who climbed with Corti was Riccardo Cassin, holder of many first ascents on the cliffs and faces of Europe. To him, Corti was a good climber who lacked basic mountaineering intelligence. "The trouble was that he was strong, but he did not have the ability to evaluate mountains," said Cassin. "He would do foolish things like refusing to use pitons on pitches where pitons were almost a necessity. Somehow or other, his phenomenal strength always pulled him through. And he was lucky." But Corti's ropemates had a way of being commensurately unlucky.

In 1952, when Corti was twenty-four years old, he was climbing Piz Badile, a two-thousand-foot-high Italian wall with many pitches of the sixth degree. Belaying his ropemate, Felice Battaglia, in a thunderstorm, Corti felt a slight jerk on the rope and at the same time was almost blinded by a searing burst of lightning. The rope went slack; the lightning had hit Battaglia and sliced the rope in half, and he had disappeared down the precipice. Making the dangerous descent alone, Corti came at last to his companion's body. The legs were broken; the chest was crushed.

Corti grieved for Battaglia, but he showed other reactions, too. Always convinced of his mastery of the mountains, he now took the death of his comrade to mean that a sort of special Providence stood watch over him in his battles with the peaks. He explained to his friends: "I feel no guilt. Sadness, yes. But not guilt. I only feel that it was bad luck that carried Felice away, but at the same time I feel less afraid myself. I am inspired."

Two years later, Corti found himself on a rope with Carlo Mauri and Carlo Rusconi in the Crigna Mountains. Rusconi was making the trail, the others following, when suddenly he shouted, "I'm falling," and brushed within a few inches of Corti to his death. Corti's reaction was to attack more and more mountains. That same summer he went to the Dolomites in Italy and Austria, traveling on the motorbike which he had managed to buy out of his forty-five-dollar monthly salary as a truck driver. In 1955 he made a training bivouac on the Petit Dru in France, one of the most difficult faces in Europe, and the following year went back to the Dru with Annibole Zucchi. Their two-man rope had climbed one thousand feet of the face when an ice block rattled loose, hit Corti full in the face and tipped him backward. Off balance, he gnashed at his piton with his teeth, but missed it by inches. Then he did a somersault in the air and slid down the ice field on his face and chest to the bottom of the cliff, Zucchi following on his back. Seriously injured internally, his face covered with blood, Corti turned to Zucchi and said in a voice quaking with anger: "Well, do we start up again now?" But Zucchi was too badly hurt to answer. Corti summoned the last reserves of his animal strength, hoisted Zucchi to his back and carried him for two hours to a resting place below the snow line. Half-blinded by the blood flowing into his eyes, Corti stumbled to the village of Montverd and collapsed in the arms of a guide.

Zucchi and Corti went into the hospital, where Corti had a long time to brood and plan revenge. More convinced than ever of his immunity to a climber's death, his thoughts now became fixed on a sinister, deadly wall to the northwest, a wall feared all over Europe, a wall called the Eiger, which had never been vanquished by an Italian. He had met a

Swiss in the little French town of Chamonix before the assault on the Petit Dru, and the Swiss had talked for hours about the killer cliff in the Bernese Oberland, and had even obliged with a picture postcard showing the face. Now Claudio had to have the Eiger. In his seething mind, he humanized the north wall, saw it as an evil monster lurking maliciously, the summation of all the lesser faces he had already attacked. As his injuries slowly healed, first for one month in the hospital in Chamonix and then for four more months in Milan, Corti kept building his hatred. He stared at the picture postcard, at the snow fields and hanging ice fields and smooth buttresses and waterfalls, and laid his poorly motivated plans. Anger at a mountain is the first mistake.

Now it was springtime, 1957, and Corti's mission was running into difficulties. He had been keeping company with a black-haired, brown-eyed girl, Fulvia Losa. This buxom, intelligent village beauty saw a gentleness in Claudio, a tender little-boy quality underneath all the boldness of his actions. And indeed Corti, removed from the mountains, was not an unlikable person. True, he was not handsome. His thin black hair was receding, and the balding patch on the front of his head was laced with pale rock scars. His face bore what at first glance appeared to be a constant look of contempt, but Fulvia quickly learned that this was merely his facial structure, and was not paralleled in his personality. His hands were oversized; his fingers were thick; his nails showed the perpetual blackness of the laborer. His table manners were not polished; he had been too long on the mountains, and he would forget himself at table and tear open sugar sacks with his teeth, thinking for the moment that he was high on some icy face with one hand gripping the wall. His speech tended to be a rapid-fire mumble, and the Italian language was almost a stranger to him. He spoke, instead, in the dialect of Lombardy, an almost unintelligible gibberish to the uninitiated. Luckily, Fulvia spoke the Lombardy tongue too, though she was one of the rare villagers who also could talk in excellent Italian, turning her phrases with precision and good grammar. Like most Italian peasants, Claudio did not confide his secret obsessions to his sweetheart. But he was kind and generous and gentle to her, and she admired him for his quiet manner and for the way he stayed on his job, driving the truck for fifty hours every week, helping to support the elderly parents in whose home he lived. If he drove his motorbike too fast, if he sometimes seemed buried in his own thoughts, this was only the child in him, and made him even more endearing. Fulvia fell in love.

Claudio, in his somewhat inarticulate way, returned the love of this pretty girl with the flashing smile and the deep brown eyes, and they planned to be married. The only problem was that Fulvia hated mountain climbing as much as she loved Claudio. The attack he was planning on the Eiger north wall would have to be kept a secret from her.

To make matters more difficult, from Corti's point of view, he could not find a partner for the climb. Wherever he went, his reputation as death's companion went before him. A hush would fall over the Lecco climbing club whenever he entered; he was hard put even to find ropemates for his Sunday workouts in the Crigna. Driving his daily truck route to cities like Milan, Turin, Como, Bergamo and back to Olginate, his massive hands steady on the wheel, he sometimes would gaze off to the north, toward the Oberland where he knew the mountain was waiting for him with malevolence. And he would try to figure out where he could get a partner. Mauri would not be his ropemate; Mauri knew his record far too well. Cassin now had notched a long series of glittering first ascents, and had been elected president of the Lecco section of the Club Alpino Italiano;

he would only have laughed at the idea of risking his life on the Eiger with so unpolished a climber as Corti. Zucchi had dropped out of touch after the fall on the Petit Dru. Rusconi and Battaglia were dead. Looking at the dog-eared postcard of the north wall which he carried constantly in his wallet, Claudio's frustration grew, and so did his smoldering anger.

April of 1957 came, and now Corti had reached the point where he was tapping climbers on the shoulder during his weekend outings, and asking them if they would go with him to the north wall that summer. One Sunday he ran into a lone figure in the Crigna. It was Stefano Longhi, fellow member of the *Ragni,* the Lecco section of the Club Alpino Italiano. Corti knew the other man only slightly, but this did not deter him from asking the usual question. To his amazement, the forty-four-year-old Longhi accepted. The improbable rope of Corti and Longhi— "Short" and "Long"—was created.

Stefano Longhi could show no important accomplishments on his climbing record, and almost no experience on ice. He was a bulky man, as European mountaineers go, standing five feet eleven inches and weighing almost two hundred pounds. He was strictly a weekend climber, working the rest of the time in a wire-and-cable factory. Quick to smile and regarded in Lecco as an extremely likable human being, he was, like Corti, not overly intelligent, and his sudden decision to join forces with Corti was strongly influenced by the simple fact that he was getting along in years and had never climbed a mountain of more than ten thousand feet. If he had any asset for an attack on the Eiger, it was merely that he had known some Swiss climbers visiting Lecco, and had picked up a little Schweizerdeutsch. But to Corti, now totally on fire with his plan to become the first Italian to climb the north wall, Longhi was sufficient.

The two huddled in the Crigna that first afternoon and

laid some preliminary plans. They decided to carry out their attack with the same secrecy which traditionally had accompanied all serious attempts on the Eiger north wall. For twenty days, they would train in the early mornings before work, and all day every Saturday and Sunday, but completely apart and on different mountains. During this period, they agreed not to be seen together.

Three weeks later, they met in a coffeehouse, discussed their capabilities, and cross-examined each other on what they had learned about the problems of ice climbing. They topped off their training with five days of climbing together in July. Now Corti asked for his summer vacation and told a tearful Fulvia that he was going off to make some safe, easy climbs in the mountains nearby. Longhi wangled two weeks leave on the technical excuse that his father had died the month before.

On August 1, a national holiday in Switzerland, they arrived by rail at Interlaken, transferred to another train up the valley of the Lütschinen and rode to Lauterbrunnen where they switched to the railway that labors up through the lower ranges to the Kleine Scheidegg hotels, across the meadow from the base of the north wall. From there they made their last change, to the tiny cogwheel railway which climbs to the yoke of the Jungfrau and the highest railroad station in the world. Just before the train enters the four-mile tunnel hacked through the interior of the Eiger and the Mönch, it stops at a small hotel called the Eigergletscher, off to the side of the north wall. Here the two Italians detrained, hauled out their climbing gear and provisions and checked in for a good night's sleep.

The next afternoon Corti and Longhi, trying to appear as inconspicuous as possible, walked across the glacier and the meadow and deposited all their climbing gear in a cache below the wall. For hours they roamed back and forth along the rock-pocked base of the cliff, seeking the most

promising route upward. The measure of their naïve drive
and blind compulsiveness was that neither had bothered to
buy one of the dozens of different maps of the face, showing all the routes taken both in failure and success. They
reckoned—as Corti always had—that brute force would
vanquish this mountain just as it had the others. Climbers
with powerful muscles did not need maps or special helps.
And hadn't it long ago been established that whatever happened on a mountain, Claudio Corti would come away
alive? No matter that Longhi was paunchy and middle-
aged, the oldest man ever to attempt the north wall; Corti
would protect his comrade on the rope.

Now Claudio made a rough pencil sketch of the route
he had selected, and both men returned to the little track-
side hotel for their pension supper of pea soup, Bernese
sausage and strong coffee. As night fell, they handed their
wallets and passports to the concierge and went to bed. At
4 A.M., they put on their climbing clothes and quietly
headed for the wall. Their food supply, brought with them
from Italy, consisted of three cans of fish, two cans of jam,
two tins of honey, two tins of instant coffee, four packages
of tea, four pounds of sugar, a pound of ham, a pound of
lard, two pounds of dried prunes, a pound of dates, five
rolls of biscuits and a pint of cognac, plus a little alcohol
cooker and a quart of fuel. Their climbing equipment was
fifteen ice-pitons, twenty-five rock-pitons, thirty-five snap
links, two ice axes, three nylon ropes of 130 feet each, two
bivouac sacks, two pairs of crampons and a small supply of
medicines. It was the bare minimum that any two-man rope
would need, along with uncommon skill and luck and good
weather, to mount the north wall.

With Saturday's dawn barely beginning to dapple the
eastern sky, the two Italians carefully picked their way
through the rockpiles and crevasses along the bottom of the
cliff, and finally set foot on the mountain. At first, the going

was easy, up a gradually steepening concave rise strewn with boulders and smaller stones. Then the wall began to flatten nearer to the vertical, and the two climbers came on what to them was an encouraging sight: rusty old pitons, left on the wall by previous climbers. A few feet farther up they found a climbing boot and part of an ice ax, and now they were convinced they were on the right trail.

They were, in fact, precisely on the "most direct" route, the route taken by Sedlmayer and Mehringer to their deaths, the simple, enticing and fatal line up the middle of the face. The pitons they found had been hammered into the wall twenty-two years before, by doomed men, and the climbing boot and ice ax had fallen from higher on the face in other Eiger tragedies.

As the day wore on, the ascent became more difficult, and finally they found it impossible to climb higher. They bivouacked for the night at 7 P.M., sleeping under clear skies. The next morning, while Fritz von Almen was spotting his three chamois below them, they worked their way back down, traversed to the west, and just as accidentally as they had stumbled on the wrong route, now stumbled on the right one. Climbing through a light snowfall, they succeeded in reaching a bivouac ledge just short of the Hinterstoisser Traverse by nightfall. By now the presence of many unweathered pitons had told them they were following the normal route, and they went to sleep full of confidence. At dawn on Monday, their third day on the mountain, they fired up their alcohol burner and sat down to a rock-ledge breakfast of biscuits, jam and coffee. But hardly had they started to eat when they beheld an amazing sight. Corti and Longhi were the first men to try to conquer the Eiger north wall since two Germans had fallen to their deaths a year before. Now, on Monday morning, August 5, 1957, there were four. The Italians gaped with disbelief at the two-man rope speedily approaching them from below.

CHAPTER FOUR

The pursuit of excellence drove Günther Nothdurft to the mountains. He attacked them neither with sullen anger nor with the flag-waving *Todeslieb* of his prewar predecessors from Germany. He was an orderly young man who approached each mountain as a problem to be solved, almost as though he were assaying a sort of vertical crossword puzzle, and then moved up quickly and sharply, with a minimum of wasted motion. He lived his life in the same way. Youngest son of a war-ravaged family—his seventy-five-year-old father had been blinded and his two brothers killed—Nothdurft wanted most of all to become "somebody," reckoning this as the least contribution he could make to the sad lot of his parents. By the age of twenty-two, he had finished his apprenticeship as a merchant—a "Kaufmann"—and after his summer vacation in 1957 he intended to go on to technical school to study textile engineering. He was short and wiry—five feet seven and 140 pounds. He wore his straight blond hair in one big shock with the part far to the left. He had protruding ears and a prominent nose and down-slanting eyes, and the over-all effect was that of a sad, superserious young man. But this was deceiving; he could laugh and see the bright side.

His first major climbs were on a rope with Walter Seeger, a young architect who lived, like Nothdurft, in Pfullingen, a small suburb of the south German industrial town of Rottweil. In 1954, when the two *Bergkamaraden* were not

36

yet twenty years old, they accomplished a difficult route up the icy Totenkirchl in the Wilde Kaiser range of Austria, and then knocked off several other climbs of the sixth degree in the Dolomites, the Grosse Zinne, and the icy Mont Blanc Massif of southern France. Before long, Nothdurft had completely outdistanced his friend Seeger in climbing ability, and indeed became recognized throughout Germany and Austria as one of the finest of the new generation of rock climbers, all by the time he was barely out of his teens. "He had one pace," Seeger said, "and that was full speed ahead at all times." Unlike most climbers, Nothdurft thought nothing of making difficult ascents entirely alone, belayed only by his own skill with pitons and ice ax. Once he made a solo climb of the northeast face of Piz Badile, a climb which had been soloed only once before, by the great German Alpinist Hermann Buhl, who took four and a half hours and afterward was lifted to the shoulders of other climbers in admiration. Nothdurft scampered to the top in three hours. He conquered the treacherous Yellow Arrete on the Kleine Zinne alone in an incredible forty-five minutes. But these were no mad, compulsive dashes. Always they were preceded by careful planning and weeks of training under similar conditions. Günther Nothdurft did not intend to die in the mountains.

Inevitably, of course, he would have to come to grips with the deadliest face of all: the Eiger north wall in the Bernese Oberland, 130 miles south of his home in Pfullingen. But Nothdurft was in no hurry. He polished his skills to a high shine, added to his records and his reputation, and waited until 1957, when he was twenty-two, to make his first visit to the Eiger. It was June, and en route to the mountain on his motorbike, Nothdurft stopped off in Lucerne to confer with Max Eiselin, a friend and fellow mountaineer. The two young men talked about the north wall. "He asked me if conditions were good at this time of the year," Eiselin recalled, "and I told him that it was a little too early, that there was still too much ice on the face." Nothdurft informed Eiselin that he had discussed the climb with Hermann Buhl, who had almost lost his life leading a remarkable ten-man international rope to the top of the north wall in 1952, and that they were in agreement that the best attack would be solo, "quick and safe," in the typical clean style of both. "I personally wanted to tell him that I did not agree," said Eiselin, "but I did not dare to give instructions to Nothdurft. One did not give instruction to better climbers than oneself."

Nothdurft went alone to the mountain, intending merely to study the face, climb a few of the more challenging pitches on the lower slopes, and do a reconnaissance for a later all-out assault. On a Friday morning he arrived in the Grindelwald valley, rode up on the cogwheel railway, and immediately began climbing. But his skill and his pace were such that he soon found himself high on the wall. He banged his way up the Difficult Crack, made the Hinterstoisser Traverse as though he were crossing the main street of Pfullingen, cramponed up the first ice field and almost to the second, and bivouacked cozily for the night. At 3 A.M. he awakened, intending to go a little higher. He lifted a bottle of water to his lips and suddenly found himself showered with broken glass. A fallen rock, missing his head by inches, had shattered the flask. To the careful Nothdurft, this was an omen. He broke camp, backed down the ice field, went across the Hinterstoisser on a heavy hemp rope he had thoughtfully left in place, and returned to the valley. That Saturday afternoon he motored back through Lucerne, and stopped again at the home of Eiselin. There, uncharacteristically, he rattled out a spate of words about the problems of the north wall. "It does not seem to me to be a very nice climb," he said. "It is very loose rock, and there are many objective dangers. The weather changes, it seems, every few minutes. I would call it a very ugly climb, and I would not like to go back. No, I do not go back to the Eiger." He left the long, cheap hemp rope, useful only for belaying traverses like the Hinterstoisser, with Eiselin, remarking that he would not need it again. Then he motored off to the northern canton of St. Gall to visit a girl friend on the way home, and later dropped into the Schuster Sports Shop in Munich, where he told the proprietor simply: "I have been to the Eiger north wall, and there is death in it."

Now Nothdurft made a few practice climbs with another twenty-two-year-old mountaineer, Franz Mayer of nearby Rottweil, a blond, full-faced, heavy-set man who made his living as a plasterer. Mayer had been showing much promise, and had performed brilliantly with Nothdurft on the west face of the Totenkirchl the previous winter. Eiselin summed him up: "He was not as good a climber as Nothdurft, but who was?" Mayer was, at any rate, a pleasant young man, and Nothdurft enjoyed his company enough to put aside, now and then, his own preference for solo climbing.

On July 20, a month after his virtuoso climb halfway up the wall, Nothdurft sent Eiselin a postcard inquiring about conditions in the Oberland, and especially on the Eiger. Eiselin replied that the mountain was covered with ice. At that point, Nothdurft announced that he was writing off any attempt on the Eiger, at least for the 1957 season, and planned instead a two-week climbing vacation with Mayer in the French Alps. The two young mountaineers sent their personal luggage ahead of them to Chamonix, and booked advance reservations at a small inn. Riding on Nothdurft's red "Puch" motorbike, they headed south. It was early Sunday morning, August 4, 1957. Fritz von Almen had not yet spotted his three chamois. Claudio Corti and Stefano Longhi were still roping down the mountain, trying to make up for their mistake of the previous day.

The road to Chamonix ran through Lucerne, and Nothdurft and Mayer stopped to pay a short visit to their friend
Max Eiselin. They arrived at lunchtime Sunday, but Eiselin
was away on a trip in the Oberland. His mother greeted
the visitors and asked them if they thought they might run
into Max on their travels. They said it was possible, and she
asked them to pass along the contents of a telegram from
a Viennese Alpinist; it had arrived at the house that morning. She read the message aloud:

CONDITIONS BERNESE OBERLAND EXCELLENT. HAVE JUST
CLIMBED NORTHFACE OF FIESCHERHORN. PROCEEDING TO
ALPIGLEN TOMORROW.

Mayer became extremely nervous, and began talking
excitedly to Nothdurft. The word Alpiglen could mean only
one thing: the Viennese climbers intended to attack the
Eiger north wall. There could be no other purpose in going to
tiny Alpiglen, far from the road to anywhere. Inexplicably,
Nothdurft, the man who always planned carefully ahead,
reacted enthusiastically to Mayer's suggestion: that they
take advantage of the good weather and climb the north
wall themselves. In his entire life, Günther Nothdurft had
made no such sudden turnabout, nor one so fateful. For-
getting even to take the hemp belaying rope left two months
before at Eiselin's house, the two young Germans called
their good-byes to Frau Eiselin and roared away toward the
south.

They stayed the night in a pension inn in Alpiglen, where
they purchased a postcard showing the normal ascent route,
and shortly after midnight arose to begin their assault. In
the chill of predawn, they climbed skillfully and accurately
on the proper route. By daybreak they had hauled themselves up the Difficult Crack, and soon, to their surprise,
spotted two men in bivouac above, just to the west of the

Hinterstoisser Traverse. The two Germans climbed up to the ledge, stretched out their hands in greeting, and established, through signs and a few words of Italian and Schweizerdeutsch, who the others were and what they were up to. Nothdurft pulled out the postcard of the face, and the four men gathered in a huddle to look at it. And then, watched from below on that Monday morning by Fritz von Almen, they broke camp and turned toward the Hinterstoisser Traverse.

On the following morning, Lionel Terray, more asleep than awake under his tent on the public campgrounds of Grindelwald, felt himself dimly annoyed. The Belgian accent is sometimes grating to French ears, and the particular Belgian accent intruding on his sleep was especially obnoxious. "Look there," the voice was saying. "I see them. There on the big snow field near the rock slope."

"Ah," another voice broke in. "I also see them. But there are three. Don't you see the third man?"

Terray turned over and pulled the sleeping sack around his head, but he could not shut out the increasing babble of voices, in many languages, prattling excitedly around the tent. He asked himself what all these people were watching, and as he slowly came to full wakefulness, he remembered that the day before, on Monday, a Swiss guide had told him that a rope of climbers was on the north wall. Terray shook his two Dutch companions, Tom de Booy and Kees Egeler, and the three of them tumbled out of the tent to witness a strange and bizzare sight. "The whole village of Grindelwald must be here," Terray said, "and it is just eight o'clock in the morning." And not only the villagers, but hundreds of others—tourists, skiers, climbers and campers, speaking in a half-dozen different tongues—milled around, chattering about the north wall and gaping upward through binoculars and pocket telescopes.

Terray quickly trained his own glasses on the face and picked out the silhouettes of four climbers etched against the snow. And as he watched, a gradual confusion came over him, a failure to comprehend what could be going through the minds of these insignificant upward-reaching ants. They were moving with incredible slowness, and this was hard for Terray to understand because he knew that conditions were good, at least as good as they ever were, on the wall. The ice field was pitched at about forty-five degrees, and covered with firm snow offering relatively solid footing. Ten years before, with his partner Louis Lachenal, Terray had traversed this same field at least twice as fast, and had gone on to victory over the north wall in a classically executed two-day climb which marked the second north wall ascent in history and the first by a rope of only two men. Not that Terray, despite this success, had anything but a healthy respect for the Eiger. His career had taken him four times to the Andes, four times to the Himalayas, up mountains like Annapurna, Makalu, the towering spire of Fitzroy in Patagonia, and almost all the famous walls of the Alps. And now, at the age of thirty-six, he readily admitted one thing to himself: of all his climbs, there were only two he would never be willing to attempt again: Fitzroy and the Eiger north wall. Though he and Lachenal had run up the wall in textbook fashion, they nevertheless had endured the agonies of a constant, drenching ice-drip, cannonades of stones, and one terrible electrical storm which forced them into a midday, unprotected bivouac. The storm broke, and the danger passed, but even skilled members of the famous corps of Chamonix guides like Terray and Lachenal would have been hard-pressed to hold out had it continued.

All the more strange it was, then, that the four climbers now watched by Terray were seemingly oblivious to a change in the color of the sky. The deep blue of the last few days was slowly giving way to heavy black clouds marching up the valley. There was still time for the men on the wall to beat an honorable, dignified retreat, to try the wall another day, but instead they moved upward at a toddler's pace, handling themselves on relatively safe pitches as though they were traversing sheer ice on roller skates. The biggest one, the last man on the rope, seemed especially inept and clumsy. Terray turned to his companions and said, "I do not understand. . . ." There could be no real glory in accomplishing what would be, after all, the thirteenth ascent of the wall. And no one made wild climbs for Fatherland any more. Terray looked again at the clouds, focused the glasses once more on the clumsy rope now approaching the spur leading to the third ice field, and said slowly: *"C'est de la graine de Macchabée.* They are bits of cadaver."

Max Eiselin, a slight wisp of a young man who looked hardly strong enough to lift the climbing boots in which he continually clomped around his native Lucerne, was breaking in a new car in the Oberland, stopping here and there for short climbs, and seeking out old friends. That Tuesday morning, while Terray and the others watched the wall in befuddlement, Eiselin drove into Grindelwald and learned that climbers had been spotted above the Hinterstoisser. Taking up a vantage point for himself, he saw them, a rope of four, moving with what seemed to him to be the pace of a slug. They were in the second ice field, and at the rate they were going, he said to himself, they would never make the top. Clearly, they should turn back. He watched anxiously for a few hours, then drove to the Grindelwald-Grund railroad station to try to learn the climbers' identities. At the station, he spotted a little mortorbike which looked familiar. Could it be Günther Nothdurft's red Puch? Eiselin was certain it could not be. Nothdurft, with his comrade

Mayer, was climbing at this very moment in the Mont Blanc Massif, several hours' drive to the south, having forsworn the Eiger at least for this year. The brilliant Nothdurft and the steady Mayer could never have been members of a rope proceeding as slowly and unskillfully as this one. Still, one had to be sure. Eiselin got out of his car and walked over to the bike. It was Nothdurft's.

More perplexed than ever, Eiselin spent the day with the other Alp-watchers and saw the rope finally reach the upper edge of the second ice field, halfway up the wall, and begin to tackle the sharp-edged ridge called the "Flatiron" leading to the third ice field. All afternoon, as Eiselin and the others watched, the four climbers battled the ridge, until by nightfall they had disappeared in the darkness near the "Death Bivouac" of Sedlmayer and Mehringer.

But the next morning, Wednesday, Eiselin was pleased to see the rope begin to take up a more normal pace across the third ice field. A Polish climbing team, training for a Himalayan climb and led by Dr. Jerzy Hajdukiewicz, watched from the camping grounds with Eiselin, and all were agreed that the climbers now were making good time. More encouragingly, the black clouds had scudded unpredictably away and the morning sun shone clear and bright on the frozen peaks of the Oberland. The Poles made preparations to sprint up the easier west wall of the mountain to greet the successful team with dry clothes, warm drinks and the traditional bottle of champagne. Eiselin drove to the railroad station and scribbled a note on a card. "Heartiest congratulations for the Eiger," he wrote. "I hope to see you back in Lucerne." He attached the note to the handle bars of the Puch, and then, inspired by the imminent success of his friends, drove away to make a quick climb of his own in the nearby Engelhörner.

Up at Kleine Scheidegg that same Wednesday, the fifth

day of the Italians' climb and the third day of the Germans', Fritz von Almen and a few friends watched the improved progress of the rope with pleasure, while out on the terrace of the hotel hundreds of tourists, attracted by the vertical tilt with death, queued up for peeps through a coin-operated telescope. A four-piece Alpine band squealed out the polkas and *shottisches* which assail the ear of the vacationer, and black-coated waiters scurried about with *apéritifs* and open-faced chicken sandwiches. With the rope now moving well, the atmosphere was festive, and optimism had replaced morbidity as the mood of the morning. But only of the morning. In the early afternoon, the sky turned gray again, and the climbers slumped back to their tedious pace of the day before, using up all the remaining hours of daylight to climb a few rope-lengths up a cliff to a bivouac site. As darkness dropped over the mountain and the first uneasy rumbles of thunder sounded from the north, von Almen began to sense disaster.

CHAPTER FIVE

A few hours after the Kleine Scheidegg telescopes were covered over on Wednesday night, a handsome young couple knocked at the door of a climbing hut on the nearby Wetterhorn. The Bernese guide who lived in the hut was in the middle of a long diatribe, which he interrupted only long enough to admit the climbers: Robert Seiler, a metal fabricator and expert amateur Alpinist from Böningen, near Interlaken, and his wife, also a skilled mountaineer. They intended merely to sleep in the refuge and resume their short climbing vacation in the morning. But there was no sleeping against the sound of the enraged voice of the guide, who now was continuing his invective. "Snots!" he was shouting to the few other climbers in the hut. "That's exactly what they are. Snots!"

Seiler, a short, chunky man with dark brown heavy-lidded eyes which made him look sleepy all the time, could not keep himself from politely asking the hut-watcher to mind his language. There was, after all, a lady in the hut, and the guide was using even more colorful phrases as his anger mounted. Now he turned on Seiler. "You don't even know what we are talking about," he shouted, "and you should mind your own business!"

"I only ask you to watch your tongue," Seiler said. "It is not the place of a mountain guide to talk like that."

But the guide ignored him. "These foreigners," he said, "climbing all over the north wall. *Schnuderbübe!* Snots! All of them! They come here and we warn them and they

46

don't take our advice. And we have to risk our lives to save them. Well, I would not do it! They have been warned and let them take the consequences." Slowly it dawned on Seiler that there were climbers on the Eiger and that this was what had set off the guide's vituperation. He sought some sober intelligence, but the hut-watcher would not stop ranting. Finally, Seiler, vexed beyond endurance, turned to him and said: "Why do you talk so much about things you do not understand?"

Said the guide: "And what do you know about all this? You are not a guide. Would you risk your life to do what we have to do, to take those people out of the wall?"

"I think I would, and I think I would behave myself far better on the north wall than you."

The guide laughed derisively. "How funny that is, coming from you," he said. "You will never have to go to that devilish place. You probably don't even know where it is."

"Even if I didn't know where it was," said Seiler, "I think I could find my way there better than you."

Robert Seiler had already found his way to the Eiger north wall seven years before, when he and three Swiss comrades had conquered the face despite a raging blizzard which overtook them on their fourth day and forced a grueling twelve-hour ascent, piton by piton, up the scarlike "exit cracks" to the summit. In those days, too, Seiler had known the sharp tongues of his fellow Bernese Oberlanders and had felt the contempt they reserved for those who attack the north wall. A few weeks before the successful ascent, Seiler had started up the wall and soon found himself trapped in a storm. He beat his way to the Stollenloch—an opening into the cogwheel railway tunnel—and lowered himself to safety. Thankful for his narrow escape, Seiler began to walk down the tracks to Eigergletscher. A sector guard halted him, learned what had happened, and ordered the exhausted climber to walk *up* the tracks to the

Eigerwand station and wait for the next train. There, despite his protestations that he had little money, Seiler was ushered into a first-class compartment for the trip down. As a final gesture of derision, the conductor refused to accept the fact that Seiler was himself a Bernese Oberlander, and denied him the automatic 25 per cent fare reduction granted to all the local residents. Ever since then, Seiler's sympathies had been with the men who climbed the wall, in victory or in death, and against what he regarded as the narrow prejudices of the others. More than most men, Seiler knew that the guides of the Lauterbrunnen and Grindelwald valleys, though brought up in the heroic tradition of their fathers, had made precious few rescues on the Eiger, had bungled others, and for many years had turned their backs entirely on the mountain.

Now, huddled with his wife in the climbing hut on the Wetterhorn, Seiler heard the whistling winds of a storm front bearing down on the Oberland. Tossing fitfully in his sleeping bag, his thoughts returning again and again to the climbers high on the face, he awoke his wife and announced that they would leave at dawn for the Eiger.

When the Seilers reached the Kleine Scheidegg hotels on Thursday, to join Fritz von Almen at the telescope, a light rain was falling. But once again the expected storm had held off, and visibility was good, except during an occasional shower. But Seiler was not complacent about the weather. He knew that a little mist down in the valley could mean a violent storm on the face, and that dainty puffs of cloud which sailed lightly over the roofs of the ski-resort hotels would often slam into the Eiger wall and discharge their loads of snow and sleet in intense miniature tempests. Peering through von Almen's double-barreled telescope, Seiler found himself baffled over the chances of the climbers. They were making slow progress, but they were on a ramp which presented fierce problems like waterfall and chimney climbs. Seiler now knew that they had already been on the mountain for at least five days, and that they had had to endure no fewer than four uncomfortable bivouacs, several drenching rain- and snowstorms, and periods of bitter cold. As each day went by, the chances of any climbing team, however skilled and experienced, diminished sharply. To make matters worse, they were now approaching the most critical single problem on the face: the so-called White Spider. To approach this near-vertical, hanging ice field with weakness, Seiler knew, would be almost automatically disastrous. The Spider was a sort of concentration point for all the problems of the Eiger. Long finger-like gullies converged into it from above, and every avalanche and rockfall was channeled through the gullies and down across the Spider's face. Now and then the snow and ice would pile up in delicate equilibrium on the Spider; a single step by a climber could upset the balance and send the entire rope spinning five thousand feet down the mountain on the back of an avalanche.

And yet the Spider could not be avoided. One climbed straight up to the left of it, hoping against hope that there would be a clear route to the summit, but always this hope was dashed by giant prison walls in the form of overhangs and ridges. The only way out was a traverse to the right, across to the Spider, and a climb through that treacherous area into the "exit cracks" running, like the face of a steam radiator, up to the summit snowfield. Nor were these exit cracks a routine problem. It was in them, seven years before, that Seiler and his rope-mates had almost met death. Continual slides of rocks rattled down the mountain alleys. One had no place to hide; one could only cover up, huddle against the side of the crack, and hope for good luck.

Watching the climbers, Seiler wondered if there was enough good luck in the whole world to see them through these dangers. By now he knew that two of the climbers were Günther Nothdurft and Franz Mayer, first-class Alpinists from Bavaria. But who was the red-jacketed man who went first on the rope, often making wrong turns and having to backtrack, and who was the other red-jacketed climber bringing up the rear, moving with awful slowness, continually being belayed and pulled to safety by the others? Seiler and his wife hiked across the meadow to the base of the wall, looking for clues to the identities of these two. But there were no tents or other signs. They came back to the hotel and told von Almen they would stand by at their home in Bönigen if help was needed.

All afternoon, Fritz von Almen watched and worried. The rope had come almost to a standstill. Through the entire day, von Almen could count only a few rope's lengths climb by the four plainly exhausted men. Late that afternoon the famous Alpine pilot Hermann Geiger made a pass in his little Piper airplane across the face. He reported that the climbers waved at him, and appeared to be in good physical condition. Nevertheless, von Almen, who had watched and analyzed almost every climb on the north wall and who was an expert mountaineer himself, was forced to the conclusion that the rope had now reached the point where its chances of success were almost nil. But what to do about it? He knew the policies of the local guides and the Bernese government about rescues on the face. Already the chief of the Grindelwald rescue section, Willi Balmer, had made several pronouncements to the effect that nothing could be done for the climbers. The only hope lay with the proud amateurs like Seiler. Von Almen went into his office and placed a call to Bönigen. "Seiler?" he said when the voice came on. "They are going to need help."

"All right," said Seiler. "Let's start something."

Thus began, for Seiler, a six-hour marathon of rounding

up, by telephone, his own coterie of elite climbers. It was the holiday season, and some of them were away. Seiler reached one in Chamonix, another in Marseilles, others in the resorts of Switzerland. To a man, they agreed to drop everything and meet Seiler the next morning at the airport in Interlaken, where planes of the Swiss Air Rescue Service would fly them up to the meadows below the face. As a final step, Seiler sent telegrams to German and Austrian climbing clubs, tersely outlining the problem and asking for help.

After a few hours' sleep Thursday night, he drove the few miles to the Interlaken Airport, now shrouded in early morning fog. One by one his comrades arrived, but no planes. For miles around, every airport was "socked in" with subminimal weather conditions. And the north face of the Eiger was completely hidden in cloud. Anxiously, the group waited around the airport for the arrival of the rescue planes.

That same Friday morning, an enterprising Bernese journalist named P. W. Bonnot, reading and digesting the sketchy dispatches from reporters now at the Kleine Scheidegg hotels, came to the same conclusion as Fritz von Almen, that the rope was doomed without outside help. He got in touch with Seiler and his comrades at the airport in Interlaken, and learned what they were up to. Bonnot was pleased by the enterprise and courage of the Seiler team, but at the same time he wondered what they could accomplish. They had only the usual ropes and ironmongery of cliff climbers. They might be able to get to the top of the Eiger by the easier west wall route, but after that they would face the awful problems of getting down to the four men, hundreds of feet below the summit, and somehow bringing them back up to safety. This had never been accomplished, or even attempted, and appeared to be suicidal to Bonnot even in the most favorable weather. He told Seiler to stand

by, made a few phone calls, and finally established contact
with Erich Friedli, an experienced rescue-service chief and
equipment expert who lived in Thun, near Interlaken.
Friedli, a stolid, courageous man with the built-in Swiss
preference for doing things by the numbers, told Bonnot
that it would be irresponsible for him to make his cables and
radios and other rescue devices available to people who did
not know how to use them and might succeed only in com-
pounding the disaster. He said he would turn over the
equipment only if the trained rescue crew from the base at
Thun was called in to assist. They agreed that Bonnot would
drive to Thun, pick up the equipment and rush it to the
airport at Interlaken, where Seiler and his men would load
it on the Swiss Air Rescue Service planes for the flight up
to the base of the wall. While Bonnot was en route, Seiler
telephoned Friedli from the airport and asked if Friedli
would be cooperative.

"Of course," said Friedli, "but I must insist that you use
my twenty-one-man crew when you operate this rescue
equipment."

"I would be most pleased," Seiler said, "but I have to tell
you I cannot promise any money or expenses. We are doing
this on our own and bearing our own expense."

"We do not care about money," Friedli answered. They
ended the conversation with the agreement that Seiler
would call back later and tell Friedli where the two crews
should rendezvous for the rescue attempt. A little later,
Bonnot arrived in Thun, loaded the cables and drums and
rollers in his car, and left for the airport. Waiting for his
crew to show up, Friedli placed a call to his counterpart
rescue chief in Grindelwald. Willi Balmer's wife answered
and reported: "Grindelwald is not doing anything because
it is impossible up there."

By Friday, the four climbers had been visible on the face

for five days; all Europe was watching the drama, and even the *New York Times* took note that four climbers, two of them believed to be Germans, were in difficulty on the wall. Journalists peered through von Almen's telescope, scribbled notes and raced to the two hall phone booths in the hotel to dictate vivid reports. Tourists from every corner of Switzerland converged on Grindelwald and Kleine Scheidegg to take an upward glance at the prospect of death; they milled around the meadow and completely filled the terrace of the hotel.

In Germany, reporters called on Günther Nothdurft's father, and extracted a quote. "My son will make it," the blind old man said simply, even as he was making preparations to go himself to Grindelwald. Back in Olginate, Fulvia Losa read the first reports of the troubled climbers on the wall, and thanked God that her Claudio was safe in the mountains nearby.

CHAPTER SIX

Four days earlier, on Monday morning, Claudio Corti had had mixed thoughts about the German rope preparing to follow him and Longhi in the attack on the Hinterstoisser Traverse. Company was not always welcome on the mountains; Corti's planning had been based on a rope of two men who knew each other's techniques and capabilities and would not be distracted by the problems of others. But, on the other hand, he had watched the approach of the two Germans with admiration; their piton-work had been sure and precise; they had wriggled up difficult pitches with solid strength and impressive technique. And they seemed, withal, to be modest, soft-spoken young men. The one whom he learned to call Franz spoke a little Italian; Longhi had his few words of Schweizerdeutsch, and all of them knew the universal sign language of the mountains. They even managed to make each other laugh, with a few light remarks and whistlings in the dark, as they stood together in the bivouac on the morning of their meeting. Then they agreed to go on with the climb in a style which had become traditional on the Eiger whenever unendangered parties chanced to meet: as separate ropes. Corti and Longhi went first, and found the Hinterstoisser free of ice and less challenging than they had expected. Corti, belayed by his partner, pounded in a trail of four pitons; Longhi followed on the traversing rope, and the Italian team left the pitons in place for the Germans to follow.

All that Monday, the two parties had worked within

close distance of each other, but as separate units. At this stage of the climb, strength was high all around, and since neither team was inclined to add to the perils of the mountain by engaging in an insane, meaningless race to the top, they remained together. By 8 P.M., they had made a careful ascent up the seventy-foot crack at the end of the traverse, cramponed across the first ice field, climbed a sheer cliff of two rope-lengths, and made their way through a few watery pitches to a bivouac site. Corti motioned to the Germans to set up their camp on a rock ledge just big enough for their two-man tent. Six feet away, the Italians nailed their own sleeping sacks to the wall with three pitons and slithered into them for an attempt at vertical sleep. Nibbling a snack and glancing down at the two thousand feet of emptiness below, Longhi confided that he was beginning to wonder if he had attempted too much, that he might not have the stamina to keep up with the younger men. It was not that he was afraid, Longhi carefully explained. But perhaps they should keep the idea of retreat firmly in mind. Corti argued that a retreat would be just as dangerous as a climb to the summit, a dubious point, but one which Longhi lacked the knowledge to dispute. Still expressing misgivings, but apparently resolved to go on, Longhi fell into an exhausted half-sleep, and Corti soon joined him.

At 3:45 A.M., Tuesday, the climbers awoke, and came together on the Germans' ledge for breakfast. Corti pounded two pitons into the ice of the wall and put the alcohol cooker on them to make coffee. Longhi broke out some jam and biscuits, and the two Italians began to eat. On the other end of the ledge, the two Germans sat watching. After a few minutes the Germans still had made no move to prepare a breakfast. "And you," said Longhi to them, "don't you eat?"

"No," said Mayer. "We haven't anything." A hurried conversation in several broken languages and a pantomime exhibition by Nothdurft soon established what had happened. Before going to sleep, Nothdurft had put the Germans' food sack under his sleeping bag to level it on the slanting ledge. Around midnight, he had felt cold, and got up to move around. It was then he discovered that the food sack had slipped down the wall. All of this he recited in a matter-of-fact way, as if it made little difference, as if they were going to get to the top so fast that it could be done without food, and most of all as if they did not want to trouble their new found comrades. Corti said, "Take," handed the Germans some biscuits spread with Italian honey, and poured them cups of strong coffee. A half hour later, the two ropes struck their camp and began an attack on the second ice field. Corti and Longhi again went first; they had been first on the mountain, and there was plenty of room for the Germans to pass them if they insisted. Longhi's pace was markedly slower on that Tuesday morning; he seemed intimidated by the wall, cut out unnecessarily large steps in the ice, and picked his way with infinite care. Corti was impatient; if they traversed this easy ice field so slowly, how could they possibly conquer the far more trying pitches above? They would need their strength, and every hour spent on the concave face only added to the cumulative fatigue which was just as much a peril on the north wall as blizzard and avalanche and rockfall.

The Germans started strongly, moving with steady pace through firm snow. But after a short time, Corti was surprised to see them slow to a snail's pace. Could this be the same two men who had flashed up the mountain like sprinters the morning before? Leading Longhi through the first part of the ice field, Corti wondered what could be happening. At five-thirty in the morning, about an hour after the day's climb had begun, Mayer shouted and gestured ahead that Nothdurft had a headache and stomach trouble. Pacing themselves so as to stay within easy climb of the ailing German rope, Corti and Longhi slowly traversed the field. By afternoon they finally reached the spur leading to the third ice field. There Nothdurft and Mayer called for assistance. The climbers linked up as a rope of four and at six o'clock quit for the night atop the spur. The hurried bivouac was a trial by water. The four men stood on a ledge less than a foot wide, only partially sheltered by a boulder. All through the night, they held their upright positions while water slopped across the boulder, soaking their clothes and filling up their boots. Standing there in icy discomfort, harnessed to rope and piton, they discussed the situation. Again, Corti argued that it made no sense to go down, no matter how ill Nothdurft was. Corti told them, as he had told Longhi, that it was easier and safer to go up. They would rope up again as a team of four in the morning, he said. He would go first, with Mayer next, Nothdurft in the protection of third position, and the two-hundred-pound Stefano providing a solid anchoring at the end. Nothdurft would feel better; Corti had given him medicine, and stomach cramps could not last forever. The Germans bravely agreed to go on.

They started climbing again on Wednesday morning over a sea of mist which shut out the valleys below. Soon they were well onto the third ice field; the mists cleared away, and it began to look as though Corti had been right. Nothdurft, though seized with occasional spasms of pain, climbed doggedly. But after they had cleared the ice field and started up a narrow cleft hard against a high wall of stone, the sickness returned more strongly than ever. And to make matters worse, Longhi now began to show signs of extreme fatigue. Five days on the mountain were telling on the forty-four-year-old man; his customary smile and good spirits had dissipated. Corti ordered a stop.

The Wednesday night bivouac, at the top of a cliff and just to the side of a waterfall pitch two-thirds of the way up the mountain, was worse than the previous one. There were occasional rains to add to the water dripping down from the snow fields above, and the spatter of the waterfall came at them sideways as they huddled close together for warmth all through the long night.

At 7 A.M. Thursday, Nothdurft was feverish and in pain, and Corti gave him several cups of strong, sweet coffee. The weary Longhi, by now not much better off than the sick German, said he was ready to go on, and the team began its attack on the waterfall pitch, one hundred feet straight up against a heavy flow of icy water. It was 10 A.M. before they had roped the last man through the drench. Now as they stood above the falls, changing into dry clothing, Corti began to have his first doubts about their chances, though he did not confide them to the others. Still ahead lay a difficult traverse, then the dreaded White Spider, the exit cracks, and the summit snow field. And they were making every inch at great expense, with an increasingly sick ropemate, and a worn-out man at the anchor position.

By noon they were ready to begin the traverse leading to the Spider. In an effort to reach the hanging sheet of ice at a higher level and thus avoid some of the avalanche danger, they had gone too high on the mountain for the normal approach—"The Traverse of the Gods"—and were forced across an icy ledge angled at seventy to eighty degrees. After four hours, they had made only six rope-lengths. Suddenly, a plane buzzed by the face. Not knowing what else to do, they waved weakly. The Spider was in sight, but high winds began to whistle around the wall, and blowing snow lashed their faces. Just to their right, they could hear the roar of the mountain artillery funneling through the center of the Spider. Nothdurft, white-faced and panting, stopped often to hold his stomach and groan, and Longhi's breathing was coming quick and hard as he followed the others across the ledge. Corti decided to call for an early bivouac in an attempt to get some sleep for a last strong dash in the morning. The bivouac was bad, but not so bad as the others; there was at least room for the climbers to sit. But the temperature dropped to fifteen degrees, and now Longhi developed frostbite. For hours through the coldness of the night, on the narrow ledge a thousand feet beneath the summit, Corti and Mayer massaged the numbed hands of their ropemate with alcohol, while Nothdurft, pale and trembling, sat off to one side, every now and then doubling up with pain.

At 6 A.M. Friday, the brave Longhi, severely weakened and with hands still dead with chill, took up his position of last man on the rope. Nothdurft, after two shots of Coramine, a stimulant, announced that he was ready. But in a few minutes, Corti could see that the rope was nearing the limit of its capacities. Longhi required almost constant attention as they slipped and clambered toward the region of the Spider. He cried out to Corti that he could not feel his hands; he was clumsy with the snap links, and barely was able to carry out his simple but important task of retrieving the pitons which would be sorely needed later in the exit cracks. Nothdurft, for his part, went along the icy traverse without complaint; but his strength was so sapped by fever and cramps that he sometimes needed help merely to open a snap link. Now they were moving inch by inch at so high a cost that even Corti was convinced that there was little hope for them. His mind flashed back to the memory of the plane the day before. It had appeared without warning, and they had not had time or presence of mind to signal that they were in trouble. Corti hoped that their weak waves had been interpreted as a call for assistance, though he doubted it. In any case, everyone knew that the Swiss guides no longer attempted rescues on the face. Corti summoned his strength, waning even in his own powerful, elastic muscles, for a final push. Perhaps if they could get through the Spider, he and the uncomplaining Mayer could force to the top and seek help for the others. Enveloped in a white cloud, the rope inched slowly ahead.

CHAPTER SEVEN

The ranking authority on Alpine rescues was shaving at that moment in his little home in Munich, 150 miles to the northeast. Ludwig Gramminger had been hauling the living and the dead off mountains for nearly thirty years. He had invented dozens of rescue devices: winch-and-cable equipment for lowering rescuers down mountainsides, brakes and pulleys for controlling the descents, a back-pack harness called the "Gramminger-Sitz," in which injured or unconscious climbers could be hauled to safety by others. Gramminger and his men had been at the Eiger twenty-two years before, when Sedlmayer and Mehringer died, but a blizzard cut short their mission. Two years later, they had returned as a sort of ambulance corps for other Austro-German ropes on the face. Now Gramminger was fifty-one years old, leader of the most renowned Alpine rescue group: the Munich Mountain Guard of the German Red Cross. A short, merry troll of a man, with one eye, a flowing mane of wavy gray-brown hair and the bulging leg muscles of a master climber, Gramminger had dedicated his life to saving others, traveling all over Europe in his little Volkswagen "Kombi" station wagon with the red cross on the side. He owned almost nothing; all his patents had been turned over to the Mountain Guard and the Red Cross; his lectures and training courses in Alpine rescue technique were free. It did not matter to him that many of the men he rescued had shown imbecilic judgment, and that some of his friends laughed at him and announced that mountain climbers were not worth saving.

Standing in front of his mirror scraping away at the overnight growth of beard, Gramminger listened attentively to the 7 A.M. news report over the Bavarian radio system. He stopped, razor poised in mid-air, as the announcer began to tell of four climbers in trouble on the Eiger north wall. Weather conditions were bad on the face, the voice said, and there was no hope that the two ropes could be brought to safety. Gramminger had heard those words before, but he had his own yardstick by which to make such final evaluations, and it was calibrated by special standards. Often when men said there was "no hope," they merely meant that rescue in the traditional manner—beating up the mountain by piton and crampon and carrying the victims down on stretchers—was out of the question. Gramminger knew there were more modern ways and plenty of experienced members of the Mountain Guard to carry them out. His face half-covered with lather, he ran to the phone and called the radio station. Where had they picked up this report, and who had decided there was no hope? The station gave him the name of Willi Balmer, chief of the Swiss Alpine Club's Grindelwald rescue station. Gramminger rang through to Grindelwald and confirmed that the news had, indeed, originated with Balmer. "I would like to come with my men and see what can be done," Gramminger told Balmer, "but of course it is out of the question unless you give your permission." Mountain-rescue groups did not compete with one another; posses of unwelcome would-be heroes had been known to turn the simplest rescues into blood baths of death and destruction for victims and rescuers alike. "I will let you know," Balmer said. "I promise to call you back with a decision." On the chance that his help would be welcomed, Gramminger remained at the telephone, alerting members of the Mountain Guard, and trying to arrange for a rapid passage into Switzerland. The German Air Force had a field at Memmingen, near the Swiss border to the south. Gramminger phoned, and was informed that a flight over the border of Switzerland would present insurmountable political difficulties, even if the drippy, gray weather were to clear. "Then please, I beg you, try higher up!" Gramminger said. The Air Force officer agreed to pursue the matter. An hour went by before Gramminger picked up the ringing telephone and heard the voice of Balmer, agreeing, with no show of enthusiasm, to permit the Mountain Guard to lend a hand. Nothing could be done for the men on the mountain, but if the Germans wanted to try, that was their business. . . .

Soon after, Gramminger had a more encouraging conversation with an official of the Swiss Air Rescue Service. The man knew Gramminger by reputation, and agreed immediately to send two planes to the border town of Alten Rhein to meet the Mountain Guard members and fly them to the Eiger. Now Gramminger took his portable two-way radios to the factory for last-minute checkups. At 11 A.M., his comrade Alfred Hellepart and several others arrived at the Mountain Guard headquarters and began loading the Volkswagen with gear. At one in the afternoon, with the one-eyed Gramminger at the wheel, they roared out of Munich toward Memmingen, where they picked up three more members of the rescue group, and on to Lindau for another, and then across the Swiss border to Alten Rhein. Here they were met by a representative of the Swiss Air Rescue Service with bad news. The same low ceiling and fog which had kept the Swiss planes from picking up Seiler and his men at Interlaken now would keep the planes from ferrying in the Mountain Guard. "Come!" Gramminger shouted to his comrades. "We will trust our faithful Kombi

to take us to the mountain." With the weather thickening
and rain already beginning to fall, they drove at breakneck
speed toward the passes of Switzerland.

That same Friday morning, while Gramminger hustled
around Munich and Seiler waited impatiently at the Interlaken Airport and Claudio Corti led his feeble rope across
the slickened traverse to the Spider, Fritz von Almen kept
watch at the telescope. Long hours passed, and there was
nothing to be seen through the mists. But in the afternoon
a momentary clearing of an air space through a corridor of
clouds showed that von Almen's harsh predictions had been
well-founded. One of the climbers was dimly visible; it was
the big man, the plodding one who always had gone last on
the rope. He was sitting all alone on a ledge nearly five
thousand feet up the wall, below the beginning of the traverse leading to the Spider. Above and to the west, just at the
base of the exit cracks at the upper edge of the Spider, a
reddish-colored tent was pitched, and a man wearing a black
jacket and hood sat alongside.

Hermann Geiger, whose ski-equipped Piper Cubs had
flown in all kinds of storm, defied the vacillating weather
for another reconnaissance of the face. As he glided by
the upper part of the wall, he could see the heavy-set man
frantically waving a red shirt. The marooned climber above
him waved desperately and seemed to be shouting. There
were no other signs of life on the wall.

Now the French guide, Lionel Terray, and his two clients,
Tom de Booy and Kees Egeler of the Netherlands, had returned to Grindelwald after two days of training climbs on
nearby peaks. They planned to take the cogwheel railroad
up to the Eigergletscher Hotel, and jump off from there on
some more training climbs up the ridges of the Mönch. But
the weather was bad, and as they idled the Friday away in

Grindelwald, they were reminded again of the climbers they had seen groping upward three days before. "I think by now that they are meat for the magpies," Terray told his companions. Training their glasses up on the face, they could see nothing through the clouds. But riding in the late afternoon train up to the Eigergletscher Hotel, they learned from other passengers that the climbers had been sighted, alive but apparently trapped, and that the corps of Grindelwald guides had announced that they could not be rescued. Still thinking of their plans to climb on the Mönch, the three men detrained at the Eigergletscher Hotel in a driving rain. They would eat some dinner, get a few hours' sleep, and, weather permitting, depart for the Mönch at one in the morning. The three were silent as they picked at their pension supper. Each, in his own way, was trying to come to grips with the disturbing thought that four men were exposed to this storm on narrow mountain ledges only a few thousand feet away. Egeler, the least experienced of the three, knew only that something had to be done, but he also had the good judgment to know that he himself was not qualified. De Booy, a strong amateur climber who later would make some difficult first ascents in Peru, waited for word from Terray, the man who had helped to save Maurice Herzog on Annapurna and had taken part in dozens of dangerous mountain rescues. But Terray sat curiously silent, consumed with his own thoughts, and grumpily turning the conversation, what little there was, away from the tragedy taking place on the Eiger.

"The world of climbers," Terray was saying to himself, "is not so nice as some people think. There is so much jealousy." His mind went back to a year before, to a drama high on the Mont Blanc, which shadows Terray's home in Chamonix. Two climbers had become marooned beneath the summit. The president of the Chamonix Society for Mountain Rescue studied the situation and decided that no help could be brought from below. The authorities called in military helicopters to make the rescue. As one of them hovered over the two climbers, rotors churning up a blizzard of snow, the pilot became dazzled and blinded, and the aircraft crashed on the mountain. A team of military climbers reached the scene, made the two weakened Alpinists comfortable in the wreckage, and guided the pilot and his crewmate to safety, promising to return the next day to bring out the others. Terray arrived in Chamonix in the middle of the ill-fated operation, and expressed surprise that no rescue parties had been formed in the valley. He quickly called together a team of his own, and headed up the peak. Now more military men got into trouble, and new rescue parties had to be sent out to save them. Terray and his crew, after one grueling bivouac, were forced down the mountain by bad weather. The result of the entire fiasco was the unnecessary deaths of the two climbers waiting in the helicopter. Said Maurice Herzog: "Mountaineering is in mourning." For his own heroic attempts to bring aid to the two dying men, Terray found himself attacked and vilified by the very guides who had cavalierly turned over their own traditional responsibilities to the military. They said that Terray had gone up the mountain seeking publicity.

All this spun through the mind of "the good angel of Annapurna" as he sat morosely at the dinner table of the Eigergletscher Hotel. By now, he knew that rescue attempts were underway; Robert Seiler and a team from the rescue base at Thun were in motion, and others were en route. Seiler had a good reputation on the mountains, and was a *Bernois* himself. Terray knew how the mountain people felt about foreigners; Seiler would be the perfect man to lead the rescue attempt; Terray would mind his own business.

But could this be his final decision? Terray began again

the anguishing circular search of his soul and his reason. And suddenly he felt himself relieved, not by his own ability to arrive at a decision, because he could not, but by the strong words of his companions. Said Egeler: "I think that Lionel should join the rescuers. That is where he belongs."

De Booy agreed. "You must, Lionel, your place is there. You must go with Seiler."

"I will go," said Terray finally, "but not as an intruder. Only if you are sure they want me."

De Booy went to a telephone and contacted Seiler. "Lionel Terray is at the Eigergletscher Hotel," De Booy said. "Do you think he can be of any help to you?"

Seiler answered without a second's pause: "I would be very pleased."

CHAPTER EIGHT

For Seiler and Friedli, Friday had been a day of frustration and confusion. Seiler's team of seven men lost the morning at Interlaken Airport waiting for Swiss rescue planes which could not land in the thick weather. In the afternoon, they gave up and drove in their cars to the Lauterbrunnen station, where only the slow cogwheel railroad offered transportation up to the wall. As they were about to board the last train, Friedli and his twenty-one-man crew drove up, and the two groups of rescuers were joined.

Now, huddled together in the railroad car as the train clacked through the culls and up the mountainside toward the Kleine Scheidegg hotels, Seiler and Friedli had to make the decision which could determine the success or failure of the mission. Reduced to simplest terms, it was merely a question of where to get off the little cogwheeler that went from the Scheidegg up to Eigergletscher Station, ducked into the long tunnel through the insides of the Eiger and Mönch, and emerged on the Jungfrau yoke, 11,333 feet above sea level. There were two choices, each presenting its own problems. They could get off at Eigergletscher and climb six thousand feet up the west wall of the Eiger to the summit. In normal weather, this climb was a routine exercise in Alpinism, and in fact was the traditional "easy" route for champagne-laden parties rushing to the top to meet successful climbers of the north wall. There were few severe pitches, and most of the route was inclined at little more than forty-five degrees.

The second possibility was to remain on the train all the

way to the end of the line, getting off at the Jungfraujoch station. Thus they would wind up four thousand feet higher than Eigergletscher, but almost two miles farther to the west. To cross this extra distance, they would have to walk east, back across the summits of the Jungfrau Massif, picking their way through several glaciers, crossing the Mönch, and finally climbing fifteen hundred feet to the Eiger summit. the question was, simply: Should they do this?

Eigergletscher Station

Or this?

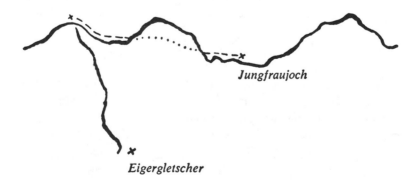

Jungfraujoch

Eigergletscher

In good weather, there would not have been two minutes' discussion. The teams would have got off at Eigergletscher and climbed the west wall. But now it was raining hard. The low-pressure area and the peculiarly Swiss "föhn" winds had brought with them higher temperatures during the day; melting snow and ice had been churning thunderous avalanches down the west wall since noon. Now the pounding rains were loosening the rock even more, and Seiler and Friedli wondered if their crews, burdened with heavy rescue equipment, would be able to survive even a forty-five-degree climb so fraught with objective dangers. The route from the Jungfraujoch to the Eiger summit, though longer and across some tricky terrain, was essentially a traverse, with a total upward reach of only two thousand feet. And since it was a higher route all the way, there was less danger of avalanche and rockfall.

"There seems little to choose," Seiler said. But they had to choose fast. There was a train waiting at the Kleine Scheidegg to make the last trip of the evening to the Eigergletscher and on to the Jungfraujoch. If they paused at Kleine Scheidegg and missed the train, they would have to add to all their other problems by hiking up through the railroad tunnel to their jumping-off point, a debilitating walk under load, even if the stubborn railroad officials would permit it, which Seiler and Friedli doubted. In the manner of an old Swiss expression, they "shook the decision out of their sleeves": they decided to go all the way up, and chance the long traverse. Late that night, they arrived at the tiny railroad station and inn nestled below the peak of the Jungfrau. From there, they made one more telephone call to Willi Balmer, and for the last time were told that no rescue attempts were planned by the guides of Grindelwald. Seiler talked briefly to de Booy on the telephone, and then the entire Swiss party, twenty-nine men in all, ranging from skilled Alpinists to short-wave radio technicians with

only routine climbing experience, turned in for a few hours'
sleep.

When Terray had resolved all his own doubts about taking part in the rescue attempts, he decided to take the train
from Eigergletscher station to the Jungfraujoch, there to
join forces with the Swiss teams. But he found that the last
train had gone. He toyed with the idea of asking the railroad
to take him up in an extra train, but he quickly discarded
the thought; he knew that the Oberland's railroaders viewed
the entire rescue attempt as an exercise in stupidity; let the
climbers work their own way off the wall, they said, just as
they had worked their own way up.

"You could walk through the tunnel," Egeler suggested.
"It is not quite four miles to the Yoke."

But Terray knew the history of the Bernese and their
Jungfraujoch Railway; it would be impossible to make the
entire climb through the tunnel without passing at least one
sector guard, and these grumpy fellows had a way of ordering interlopers to turn around and get out of the tunnel, no
matter what their mission. It was the rules, and one went
by the rules, especially when they coincided with one's own
prejudices and opinions.

Still, Terray had to get up to Jungfraujoch somehow.
"Maybe we could get you a special pass to walk in the tunnel," de Booy suggested.

"We could try," said Terray.

De Booy, a multilingual man of sophistication and charm,
approached the employees of the Eigergletscher Station,
and asked them, in their own Schweizerdeutsch, for permission. Absolutely not, said the railroaders. It was against
the rules.

Whom might he telephone for a clearance? De Booy
asked. The railroaders told him the central office was in
Bern; he was welcome to try, but they could tell him now

that it would be a waste of time. De Booy rang up Bern, spoke to several officials of the railway system, and finally reached the director himself. "Absolutely not!" the director said. *"Verboten ist verboten.* We cannot change our rules for any rescue action."

"Is that final?" de Booy asked.

"That is final, and official."

De Booy told Terray, and the Frenchman said he was not surprised. "It is typically *Bernois,*" he observed. "We will just have to get some sleep and try to catch up with the rescue team in the morning."

"But by then they will be on their way across the top," de Booy said.

Terray snapped: "Then we will have to climb the west wall ourselves." Full of distaste for the stubborn Bernese, and full of pity for the lost Alpinists on the mountain, the three men dropped off to sleep at midnight.

It was almost nightfall that Friday when Ludwig Gramminger and his comrades of the Munich Mountain Guard came to the conclusion that they would have to drive their Kombi to Grindelwald. It was raining heavily now, and the overloaded little half-station-wagon, half-bus careened around the turns as they headed into Zürich. "Say, Wiggerl!" said Hellepart, addressing Gramminger by his nickname. "I am ready and willing to face death on the mountain, but I would rather not go to my death on the highway."

"Do not worry yourself," said Gramminger, hunched over the wheel, his one good eye squinting into the transculent fog ahead. "I have made no plans to die here or anyplace else. But if we do not get to the mountain quickly, it will be too late, and everything will have been wasted."

"I was only teasing you, Wiggerl," said the affable Hellepart, a compact two-hundred-pounder who many times had dangled from the end of a Gramminger cable, trusting his life to the skill and inventiveness of the leader.

Soon the lights of Zürich and Lucerne were behind them, and they entered the Brünig Pass winding into the Oberland from the north. Hellepart shut his eyes and tried to doze as Gramminger cornered the Kombi through slanting sheets of rain, negotiating the hairpins of the Brünig as though on a track. They passed through the sleeping town of Interlaken and arrived at Grindelwald after midnight. The village was dark. The last regular train up the mountain had long since made its final run and returned to the trainshed for the night. The Munich men wondered where to turn. There may have been human beings dying far up on the wall, but the townsfolk of Grindelwald were enjoying a good night's sleep.

Max Eiselin had come down from the Engelhörner that night and checked into a hotel for a rest. He flipped on the radio in his room, and, to his utter amazement, learned that the two ropes on the Eiger had come to a standstill and rescue operations were beginning. Pulling his soggy climbing clothes over his pajamas, he ran to the telephone and called his mother in Lucerne. Yes, she said, a man named Robert Seiler had tried several times to reach him. There was some sort of trouble on the north wall. Eiselin cut the conversation short, bolted out of the hotel to his new car, and headed for Grindelwald. The resort village in the valley was dead; every available hotel was filled with sleeping tourists, many of them there to watch the morbid drama on the wall. Eiselin parked his car at the railroad station and slumped across the front seat to get a few hours' rest before catching the first train in the morning. Hardly had he begun to doze when the noise of another vehicle snapped him upright. He looked out the window and saw a small bus with a red cross painted on the side. He flagged it down and was relieved to recognize Ludwig Gramminger and several other members of the renowned Mountain Guard of Munich.

"Is there no special train?" Gramminger asked Eiselin.

"What special train?" said Eiselin.

"Why, the train to take us up the mountain. They knew we were coming. I received permission from Willi Balmer this morning."

"If you understood they would arrange a special train for you," said Eiselin, "it is strange. You can see that the station is closed for the night."

"Well, then," said Gramminger, "let us telephone to Balmer and see what goes on."

They let the telephone ring for several long minutes, but there was no answer at the Balmer residence. "Why don't we go to his house and stir him out of bed?" Eiselin asked. "If he knew you were coming here, he surely must at least have made some hotel reservations for you."

They piled into the now thoroughly overloaded Kombi and drove the short distance to the Balmer residence. After many loud knocks on the door, the rescue chief appeared, clad in a nightshirt and rubbing the sleep out of his eyes. "I am here with the Mountain Guard of Munich," Eiselin said. "What is the situation?"

"*I' weiss nüt,*" said Balmer in his thick, Oberland accent. "I know nothing."

"Do you mean to say that you have not even arranged for sleeping quarters for these people?" Eiselin asked.

"*I' weiss nüt,*" Balmer repeated. "Come in the morning and we will see what can be done."

As they drove back toward the center of Grindelwald, Eiselin felt baffled and confused. He could sympathize with the attitude of the Grindelwald guides (although he did not agree with it). Not for outsiders was it to pass judgment on men who long before had had their fill of the spectacular climbers of the Eiger and long before had decided to deter the cliff-walkers by the simple expedient of a sort of sit-down strike, a refusal to take part in any rescues on the face. But that did not explain Balmer's behavior toward the Mountain Guard. It was only common Swiss courtesy to arrange a greeting for visitors, even if they were coming merely to see the sights. No one was asking Balmer to go up the wall, but surely it was strange for him not to answer his telephone, to make no plans for a hotel, and not even to arrange a train to take the visitors on their errand of mercy to the top. Eiselin shrugged his shoulders and wondered.

Now they had four hours to spend until the first train departed in the morning, and all were fatigued—Eiselin from climbing all day on the Engelhörner, the Mountain Guard from the long journey down from Munich. Already Gramminger and his men had established that the hotels were brimming with tourists and gawkers. "Come," said Eiselin. "I have a plan." His idea was to ask for some space —a few sofas in the lobby or a hallway in which sleeping sacks could be laid out—in the Hotel Glacier near the rail-road station. But all the knocking and shouting in the world could not awaken the concierge. They walked around to the back and spotted some open windows. Eiselin was hoisted to the shoulders of a Municher. Inside, he could see a sort of dormitory where a group of Girl Scouts were asleep with a few adults. He dropped over the transom and landed on the stomach of a sleeper. When the commotion had subsided, and explanations had been made all around, the weary expeditioners climbed through the window one by one, doubled up in a few empty beds, and prepared for a short sleep. It was now nearly 3 A.M., Saturday, August 10. Gramminger set his wrist alarm for six.

CHAPTER NINE

Balancing across the narrow, ice-encrusted traverse toward
the White Spider early Friday morning, Corti had pounded
a trail of pitons in the wall, but he had faith neither in the
stability of the rotten rock nor the capacity of the sick
Nothdurft and the frostbitten Longhi to hang on much
longer. Almost at the Spider's edge, he hammered a last
piton in, attached a snap link to it, and passed the rope
through the link and over his left shoulder so that he could
belay the two Germans as they came cross to him. The
climbers were positioned like this:

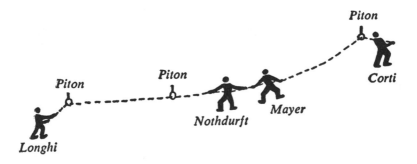

The Germans moved to a position about fifteen feet from
Corti and slightly below him, and now Corti shouted to
Longhi to knock out the last piton and move up to the next.
The older man was out of sight behind a slight bulge, but
he was obeying instructions; Corti could measure Stefano's

progress by the slackening of the rope as he took it in inch
by inch until about ten feet were coiled around his chest.
And then, almost precisely at the instant Ludwig Gramminger was switching on the 7 A.M. news in Munich, Corti
heard a scream.

"*Volo!* I am flying!" Then: "*Tienimi!* Hold me!" Automatically, Corti braced for a jolt. The rope dug into his left
shoulder and tore through his hands with a force so intense
that he could feel deep burns being scored into his palms
through the climbing gloves. With all his strength and
weight, he squeezed the slipping rope with his injured hands
until it slowed, and stopped. Carefully, without daring to
take a breath, Corti turned his head and looked across the
precipice. Ninety feet below the second piton, penduluming
helplessly back and forth in a wide arc, was the form of his
comrade Longhi. Corti held fast until the motion stopped,
secured the rope and asked the two Germans to belay him
as he inched back across the traverse to a point directly
above the limp Longhi. There he was relieved to hear his
comrade call, "Claudio! Let me down. There is a ledge
below me. Drop me to the ledge!" Slowly, Corti let the rope
slide through his burned hands until, at last, it slackened.
"I am on the ledge!" Longhi called. Now the problem was
to get him all the way back up.

"What happened, Stefano?" Corti shouted down the face.

"My frozen hands, they would not hold any more."

"How are you doing now?"

"My hands are cold. I cannot feel them. They are frozen.
I cannot even use them to attach the ropes to the wall."

Corti called to the Germans, holding tightly to the rope
to protect him in case he fell from his own improvised
stance. He asked them to belay him while he tried to get to
Longhi. Then he began lowering himself on the ice slope.
From the beginning, it was a perilous belay. Nothdurft desperately tried to maintain his own stance on a ledge a few

inches wide; Mayer had to keep a constant watch on his German comrade and at times found himself belaying both men as Nothdurft slumped into the rope. Corti went down to an outcropping about sixty feet above Longhi, but further progress would mean a descent through open air, and not even the heroic Mayer would be able to support the free-hanging weight.

"Take me up, Claudio!" Longhi pleaded.

"Don't worry, Stefano," Claudio answered. "I will get you up."

But a few attempts at a direct lift showed immediately that the dead weight of the bulky Italian was too much for Corti in his weakened condition. The ropes were rubbing over a sharp edge of ice, and Corti could see them beginning to fray. He called on Mayer to join in the pull, but the ropes were placed in such a manner that all of Mayer's efforts only succeeded in jamming Corti's hands against the ice. It was hopeless. Corti tried to jolly Longhi into helping himself up. But Longhi's strength was at an ebb; he clawed awkwardly at the walls with his frozen hands, and could not budge upward from the ledge. "Stefano," Corti called. "How are you doing?"

"You will have to pull me up, Claudio. I cannot make it."

"How am I to do it, Stefano?" Corti asked. "I have no strength any more. The Germans are finished too." Corti knew that Longhi would have to remain on the ledge while the others tried to force a route to the top and seek assistance. There was no other way. Corti lowered his bivouac sack with the remaining food and medicine through a snap link to the ledge below. Then he shouted down:

"Stefano, I go to seek help. Tomorrow we come back to take you up. Stefano, can you hear me?"

"Yes," Longhi replied. "I'm all right. I'll wait for you."

Corti took one final look at his friend, sitting there on

the tiny ledge, his feet dangling over the wall. But he was still alive, and apparently unhurt except for the frostbite, and at least he would be able to eat and rest. Corti drove pitons into the rock bulge, and fixed to them the two ropes going down to Longhi. Now no storm or winds could blow Stefano from the wall; these lifelines would protect him. Corti shouted, *"Addio,* Stefano, *Coraggio! Coraggio!"* and began the slippery climb back up through the mists.

Longhi's fall and the attempts to haul him up had cost the rope three hours, and now it was almost ten in the morning. Clouds full of rain dashed against the face as the tiring climbers headed across the upper edge of the White Spider. Rockslides and avalanches missed them by a few feet, but after several more hours they had reached the exit cracks, penultimate problem on the north wall. Now they were only seven hundred feet from the top, and less than that from the relatively easy summit snow field. But Nothdurft was finding it tough going as he wriggled upward through the ugly rock-scoured gullies leading slantwise toward the peak. Mayer and Corti continually belayed him from above, and more than once one of them had to crawl back down to help the weakened German open a snap link. By three in the afternoon, the rope had accomplished only a few hundred feet upward into the clouds. Corti was hammering in pitons as lead man on the rope, a few feet above the others, when a rock tumbled down the face and hit him in the head. He lost his balance and fell backward, alternately spinning through space and ricocheting off the slope. He jerked up hard against the rope, sixty feet below the others, dangling head down over the hanging ice of the Spider. The blood from a long gash on his head spilled in crimson drops into the air, and he felt himself losing consciousness. "Pull!" he shouted in Italian. "Pull the rope!" After long seconds the Germans understood, and Corti was maneuvered into a vertical position. He swung on the rope, grabbed at an outcropping, and hugged himself to the wall.

Now Mayer dropped down a few feet to a more secure stance on a ledge. Hauling at the rope, he helped Corti regain the sixty lost feet. Head spinning and face encrusted with blood, Corti was now half-delirious. "We are not yet defeated by this mountain," he announced wildly. He stood up to continue the ascent, but his wobbly knees buckled under him. He mumbled out his thanks to the two Germans, while Mayer cleaned the wound with snow and bound it with muslin, and he wondered if they understood him, now that Stefano was no longer here to interpret. And then he realized that Mayer was trying to say something to him. "Tomorrow at five o'clock," Mayer was saying. He handed Corti the red bivouac tent. "Tomorrow at five o'clock," Mayer said again, and then the two Germans snapped onto the rope for the climb upward.

"They will come for me tomorrow," Corti told himself. He watched them climb ten, twenty, thirty feet. Then he saw them pause, smile wanly at him, and vanish upward in the mists.

Just after eleven that night, Robert Seiler lay in his sleeping sack in Europe's highest railroad station on the yoke of the Jungfrau, and pondered the chances of the hurriedly flung-together group. All around him were the shadowy forms of the rescuers. There were the six members of Les Bouquetins, "the ibexes," all sixth-degree elite climbers who had been Seiler's ropemates many times before. And there was Friedli, a man who ranked as an expert in the use of special rescue equipment, with his twenty-one-man team from the rescue base at Thun. Bold as they were, Seiler thought, there were some of them who had perhaps reached too far in agreeing to make the long dark traverse across the glaciers and the south flank of the Mönch to reach the summit of the Eiger. Such traverses presented problems even to strong climbers in broad daylight. But this would be worse: they would be leaving in the black of night; they would be cutting across an unmade trail covered with fresh snow; and they would be loaded down with cables, food and bivouac equipment. About Friedli, Seiler had no misgivings. The imperturbable man of Thun had acquitted himself in many previous difficult climbs and rescues. But numbered in Friedli's crew were necessarily some men who were little more than radio technicians. They would be vital to the success of the mission; when rescuers were dangled far down cliffsides on thin cables, there had to be excellent, dependable radio communications both ways, else the cable might become fouled and the rescue itself become a disaster. But could these technicians make the traverse? Perhaps, Seiler said to himself as he fought sleep, the parties had made a mistake coming so high. Already some of the men were complaining of severe headaches and lightheadedness; they had not had enough time to acclimatize themselves to the high altitude, and they were suffering from oxygen starvation. Perhaps they should have stayed at the Eigergletscher and climbed the west wall. But there had been so little time to make the decision. There was nothing to do now but move straight ahead.

Seiler's sleep was numbered in minutes that night. It was 2 A.M. when Friedli awakened him and announced tersely: "We go." They dressed hurriedly, and strapped heavy packs of material on one another's backs. Seiler and his ropemate, Martial Perrenoud, and another rope of Paul Müller and Willi Uttendoppler, were less heavily loaded; they would make the trail for the others. They stepped out the side door of the railway station and into a scene of incredible change. When they had gone to bed, a heavy rain was falling, and avalanches were rumbling down the peaks. But now a front of howling, frigid winds had moved in from the northwest, shoving the clouds away. Every star in the sky was shining brightly; icicles two feet long hung from the eaves of the building; wherever there had been water, now there was ice. It was a scene of breathtaking beauty; but it was not beautiful to the twenty-nine men who would have to make the long journey in the cold winds across the very roof of Switzerland. If there had been any doubt earlier about their choice of routes, all doubt now was gone. They had traveled up to the Jungfraujoch mainly to avoid avalanches and rockfalls on the west wall. But now every snow field and every rock was held immobile by the snap freeze; there was no objective danger whatever. A climb of the west wall under those conditions would have been routine. The icy trip across the south flank of the Mönch would be doubly difficult. Seiler cursed the unpredictable weather, and with three of his comrades, moved out into the bright moonlight.

The winds snapped at them as they fought their way across the glacier which led to the Mönch. After an hour and a half, Uttendoppler yelled and dropped from sight. He had fallen through a thin veneer of snow and ice concealing a deep crevasse, and now he was wedged tightly in the crack, only his arms and head showing. Seiler, Perrenoud, and Müller, soon joined by another rope of two men from the rear, tugged and hauled at him, but he would not budge. Losing valuable time and energy, the five men dropped their packs, grabbed Uttendoppler's arms, and slowly squeezed his pinched body out of the crevasse. Bruised and scraped, Uttendoppler insisted on going on, and the three ropes moved again into the snowless gale. After hours of dangerous maneuverings, they had passed behind the Mönch, and now they had to get up the Eigerjoch. But the winds had blown away the snow at the precipitous edge of the field; now smooth sheets of ice hung like mirrors, reflecting the cold moonlight. Together, the men banged in pitons and laid long cables for those overladen carriers who would follow. Friedli and his ropemate, Walter Stähli, who had left the starting point after the trail breakers, caught them up and went ahead to break a path. It was an agonizing journey, and many times on the way the rescuers thought how much easier the west wall would have been that morning. It was ten o'clock Saturday morning before Friedli and Stähli, fighting the winds all the way, set their feet on the icy summit ridge of the Eiger. There, hard at work hacking level areas in the tilted top of the snow field, were two strangers.

At four o'clock that morning, while Perrenoud, Seiler, and the others struggled to wrench their comrade out of the crevasse and Friedli and Stähli approached from behind, Lionel Terray and Tom de Booy were already moving up the west wall from the Eigergletscher Station. They found the route icy but safe, all danger of avalanche and rockfall held in sharp suspension by the biting winds which whipped down from the northwest in gusts up to fifty miles an hour. The two men were at the top of their form, having spent many days in training climbs in the Oberland, and they climbed in classic manner, belaying each other up difficult pitches, running on crampons across the angled fields of firm snow. De Booy, the powerful schoolteacher from Amsterdam, dogged the footsteps of the internationally famous Chamonix guide, and before two hours had passed, they were halfway up the wall. Now they could begin to see other men working their way across the ridge of the Mönch, up where the wind would hit them in a solid sweep from the north. First there were two climbers, moving doggedly, broadside to the gale; a few hundred yards back came six more, and far behind them, stretched across the high ice fields and struggling under a heavy load, came a dozen or so stragglers. This must be the Swiss party which had started from the Jungfraujoch. Terray, inexplicably, felt deep emotional ties to these brave men, some of them obviously not good climbers, as they risked their lives with each step. And for what? For nothing, Terray said to himself. There could be no life left on the north wall after such a frigid night. The most powerful climber could not have endured six or seven bivouacs on that terrible face, capped by this final bone-chilling wind. "The north wall," Terray mused to himself. "Surely there is not another place in the world so frankly hostile to human beings. There cannot be anyone alive on it." But then why had he joined the rescue party, risking once again the backbiting of those who had stayed comfortably behind in their homes in the valley? "It is because of those Swiss up there," Terry told himself. "It is because they are brave men taking a generous action." He felt again, as he had on Annapurna, the spirit of solidarity toward courageous men who ignored the odds and the probabilities in a dangerous attempt to bring relief to others who were suffering.

By seven-thirty Terray and the Dutchman were one thousand feet from the summit, and they could inch out on the ridge of flaky rock and hanging ice which separated the west wall from the north. There was no entrance to the north wall anywhere on this spur, but at least they could survey the precipice and look for the last traces of the lost rope. Terray shouted across the face, and, just as he had expected, there were no answers. For almost thirty minutes, he and de Booy took turns calling, but the only returning sound came from the wind, ripping and whistling around the fragmented edge of rock. They turned to back off the ridge and finish the climb to the summit when, faintly in the distance, they thought they heard an indistinct call. They looked up to see if it was coming from the Swiss, but those climbers seemed to be occupied with their own problems. Terray called again, and this time a voice came out of the wall.

"I cannot believe my ears!" said Terray. "There is a living being out there."

"Perhaps we are hearing things, Lionel," de Booy said. But now the calls were coming more often. They could not make out what the voice was saying, or even in what language it spoke, but they knew that it came from the wall. Inspired and touched, Terray and de Booy groped back off the outcropping and forced the rest of the climb so that they would be on time to help the Swiss who should, by now, have reached the summit. At 8:45 they came to the top, and found it as deserted as it had been ten years before when Terray, with his partner Lachenal, had climbed the north wall after two days of exhaustive effort.

Now there was no longer any lee in which to find respite from the wind, howling at gale force, and Terray was afraid that he and de Booy would be blown off the sharp edge of the summit ridge and down one side or the other. To warm themselves, and to give themselves a stable footing, they began hacking a level platform out of the ice of the ridge. They had worked for nearly two hours when the first pair of Swiss set foot on the ridge. There was hardly any greeting, and no introductions. With a few quick remarks in Schweizerdeutsch, some hurried gesticulations and an abrupt, no-nonsense manner, the two Swiss sat down alongside Terray and de Booy and began to brew tea.

CHAPTER TEN

All of the long Friday, while the Swiss teams were catching trains to the Jungfraujoch and the four-man Italo-German rope was struggling on the north wall, a little Fiat 1100 hummed its way across the valleys of northern Italy, into the Italian Alps, and through the passes into Switzerland. In it were two renowned names in international mountain climbing: Riccardo Cassin, whose first ascents of European walls filled the record books, and Carlo Mauri, veteran of Italian expeditions all over the world. They were on their way to climb the north wall. Cassin, the older at forty-eight, had been elected president of The Ragni, in testimony to his impressive record, which included first ascents of such famous walls as the north face of the Western Zinne, the northeast face of Piz Badile, and the Walker spur on the north face of the Grandes Jorasses in the French Alps. He was a short, compact man with thinning black gray-laced hair, light hazel eyes and a slightly pushed-in nose which gave him the look of a tough, little lightweight boxer. His companion, Mauri, was a heavier man, standing just a shade under six feet, with clear, blue-gray eyes, an enormous shock of unruly brown hair, and a big, friendly smile for everyone. At twenty-seven, he was in the middle of a climbing career which would take him on expeditions to Greenland, Patagonia and Chile, and up many of the major faces of the Alps.

There was, however, one face the two men had not climbed, nor had any of their countrymen. Earlier in the summer of 1957, Cassin and Mauri had made reconnaissance climbs on the Jungfrau, as training for the wall they wanted: the Eiger. They found the entire Massif heavy with ice and snow, and too dangerous. The season would have to wear on a little more. A few weeks late, back in Lecco, they heard the mountain was now ready: several days of warm, clear weather had wrenched loose a lot of soggy ice, and already there was climbing activity on the face. If the weather held, a rope might stand a chance to get up. They were on their way back to find out.

Cassin and Mauri arrived in Grindelwald late Friday night, could not find an empty hotel room, and parked their Fiat at the railroad station to wait for the first cogwheeler in the morning. Filled with the excitement of anticipation and jammed together in their cramped sleeping quarters, they had managed only a few hours' rest when the sun came through the windshield and woke them up. They stumbled out of the car to see a Volkswagen Kombi parked nearby, a red cross painted on its side, the international "D" of Germany next to its license plate. Immediately they knew that there was trouble on the face; the famed Mountain Guard of Munich did not come to Grindelwald on pleasure trips. Instantly discarding the anonymity with which they had hoped to cloak themselves until they had surveyed the mountain, Cassin and Mauri walked over and introduced themselves. Max Eiselin and Ludwig Gramminger told them that a rope of four was in trouble on the wall.

"Who are they?" Cassin asked.

"I am sure that two of them are Germans," said Eiselin. "They are Günther Nothdurft and Franz Mayer. Nobody knows who the others are. Some say they are Austrians. There is also a rumor that they are Italians."

Cassin and Mauri asked permission to join the rescue parties. Gramminger told them their help would be welcome, especially if the climbers proved to be Italians. Just

then a handsome man walked up to the group and announced that he was the leader of a group of eight Polish
mountaineers, training in the area for later climbs in the
Himalayas. "My name is Dr. Jerzy Hajdukiewicz," he said.

Gramminger introduced himself, and Hajdukiewicz said,
"I know you, I know your reputation, and I put my group
entirely at your disposal. We are well-equipped, and we are
well-trained."

"It is good," Gramminger said. "Nationality is of no im-
portance here. We can use your help."

The Mountain Guard, the Italians and Eiselin boarded
the 6:30 A.M. train for the Eigergletscher station; the Poles
would get the next train and meet them there for the climb
up the west wall. At the transfer point at the Kleine Scheidegg, where they had to unload and load again, the group
learned that Friedli and Seiler with some thirty men were
already on their way over the top of the Massif. They could
see two other climbers—Terray and de Booy—high on the
west wall, almost to the top. Inside the Kleine Scheidegg
hotel, they found von Almen talking on a short-wave
hookup to Friedli, relaying a vague report that two men
had been seen on the summit after midnight. Gramminger
came on the air and asked Friedli what was happening.
Only eight of the original party would be able to make it
to the Eiger summit by the high route, Friedli explained.
The others were forced to go back to the Jungfraujoch and
take the train down to Eigergletscher to reapproach the
summit by the west wall route. Did Friedli have rescue
equipment with him? Gramminger asked. Only a little,
Friedli responded. He had a brake, grappling irons to anchor it, some cables and some rope. But the vital couplings
to join the cables were with the men who had had to turn
back.

"Then we will bring you everything you need," Gramminger said.

By 10 A.M., the augmented Mountain Guard party had reached the Eigergletscher Station, where they began preparing their equipment and apportioning the loads for the climb up. Cassin, Mauri, and Eiselin went on ahead as a rope of three, to break a good trail for the load-bearers who would follow. They climbed quickly, benefiting by the tracks of Terray and de Booy, who by now were in clear sight on the summit ridge. By 1 P.M., the Italians and Eiselin had reached the point where the footprints of the first two slanted off to the ridge overlooking the north wall. "Perhaps they saw something," Mauri said, and the three men traced the steps to the edge of the ridge. Out on the bleak wall, they saw nothing. But they could hear a thin voice against the wind. It seemed to be calling names, the same names over and over again. Then there would be a silence, and moaning noises, and then the names again. Mauri leaned far out over the ridge and yodeled the first thing that came to his mind: the loud "RAGNI-I-I-I-I-I-I" of the Lecco club. Back from the wall, but far weaker than Mauri's yell, came an answering call, the same Ragni yodel by which the men of the Lecco club communicated with one another across the peaks of their own Crigna.

Mauri shouted: "*Chi sei?* Who are you?"

"Longhi!" the voice said. "Stefano!"

It seemed incomprehensible to Cassin and Mauri, both of whom knew Longhi well, that this bulky, friendly bear of a man, this man who had never made a major climb and who was well into his middle years, was one of the marooned climbers on the Eiger. Could they have heard the name wrong? Guided by the sound of the voice, they were able to pick out a lone figure, standing on a tiny ledge, frantically waving the red climbing jacket of the Ragni. Mauri stood straight up, so that he could be seen clearly, and then came the yell which dispelled any doubts about the identity of the marooned man. *"Bigio!"* the man called.

"*Bigio!*" This was the nickname by which Mauri, because of his blue-gray eyes, was known in Lecco.

Cassin clambered to the edge of the ridge and called, "Stefano! We have come to save you!"

"Giulio! Giulio!" Longhi shouted, mistaking Cassin for another man, a close friend in the Lecco Alpine Club.

"No," called Cassin. "It is me: Cassin. We have come to save you!"

"Come to help!" Longhi cried, his voice suddenly stronger against the wind. "*Fame! Freddo!* Hungry! Cold!"

"We will come!" Mauri shouted at the dim figure a thousand feet across the wall. With Eiselin and Cassin, he scrambled back to the upward route. For several minutes, as they resumed the climb on the difficult upper slopes, they could hear Longhi's voice calling after them: "Riccardo! Riccardo! *Bigio! Bigio!*" Then the voice died on the wind. When they reached the top at 3 P.M., they could see that the rescue party was getting ready to lower a man on a cable.

Erich Friedli, a dour man under the best of circumstances, had every reason to be in a bad mood when he and Walter Stähli finally staggered onto the summit ridge after nine hours of balancing across a slanting wall of ice and snow. His annoyance had begun long before the traverse, even before he had left for the mountain. On Friday, after the journalist Bonnot had picked up the rescue gear, Friedli had talked to Seiler by telephone and had been asked to stand by for further instructions. For several hours Friedli and his experienced rescue crew fidgeted about the base in Thun, waiting for a call which never came. Seiler had, instead, rushed ahead with his own crew of elite rescuers, bearing Friedli's rescue equipment, and followed by a few journalists who smelled a good story. It had all been merely an oversight on Seiler's part, one of those mistakes which, picked up and observed in calm comfort later, may seem to have been motivated by a desire to be first, or to "put something over." But in the context of all the confusion on that Friday morning, with Seiler waiting for planes to arrive and the Scheidegg reporting that one climber was already marooned and the others appeared to be doomed, it was not surprising that Seiler simply forgot that he had promised to call Friedli and assumed that Friedli and the rescue crew were making their own way to the north wall. It was late Friday afternoon before the Friedli group had jumped into their cars and driven to the railroad station at Lauterbrunnen, where they were just in time to catch Seiler and his crew boarding the last train. Thus there was ill feeling from the beginning. Friedli blamed Seiler for causing his crew to lose the best part of the day, at a critical time in the rescue, when every second counted and men might already be dying. And he was irked that Seiler, who had never used the cable-pulley equipment in rescue operations, had had the nonchalance to leave behind the trained men of Thun and go to the mountain himself with devices he did not know how to handle. It had not been nonchalance, of course; it had been human error. But Friedli had no way of knowing this.

Then there was the matter of the decision to climb to the Jungfraujoch. It had been no more Seiler's decision than Friedli's; they had "shaken it out of their sleeves" on the train ride up to the Eigergletscher. Nevertheless, it was a bad decision, and they were lucky it had not multiplied the disaster already taking place. Of the twenty-nine men who had left the Jungfraujoch early Saturday morning, only eight would be able to make the traverse to the Eiger roof—Friedli, Stähli, Seiler, Perrenoud and four others. The rest, after several nearly fatal accidents, had had to retreat to the Jungfraujoch, wait for the train to take them down to Eigergletscher, and start all over by the west wall route.

With them had gone valuable bits of equipment—extra lengths of cable, couplings, medicines and bivouac gear—which now would not arrive until much later Saturday. For the moment, as he brewed tea with the two strangers and caught his breath, Friedli could count on only minimal equipment—a few cables, but no couplings to extend them down to the Spider, a meager supply of small brakes and pulleys through which the cable would pass, grappling hooks and some radios which had been severely knocked about on the traverse across the Mönch.

But at least they could try. And Friedli, with every justification, had confidence in his own abilities to direct such a rescue. He was a master technician, and for many years he had devoted almost all his time to the improvement of rescue equipment and the training of crews. Many Alpinists owed their lives to Friedli and the strong climbers of the rescue base at Thun. They had even attended training courses given by the great rescue chief Ludwig Gramminger of Munich; Friedli himself had gone through two of the courses. Now braced by the hot tea and feeling stronger after a short rest on the ice platform hacked out by the two strangers, Friedli began to steer the operation with an expert's hand.

To Terray and de Booy, first up the mountain, the behavior of the two newly arrived men was inexplicable. Questioned in Schweizerdeutsch by the polylingual de Booy, above the din of several light planes now droning back and forth across the face, they slowly gave details on what was happening behind them on the traverse. They seemed to show none of the camaraderie or high spirits with which men on mountains traditionally come together, happy to see other humans after long fights alone. Instead, the two cool Bernese men picked themselves up and began hacking out a new platform and fixing cables to the unstable rock on the ridge. Immediately Terray saw that they were working much too far to the west; a cable dropped straight down from that point would miss the trapped men by at least two hundred feet. Through de Booy, he explained all this to Friedli and Stähli, but there was no response. For three hours, the impassive Bernese went about their work of preparing the cable, ignoring all suggestions.

"But I did notice," Terray said later, "that this man Friedli was an extraordinary technician. It was very obvious that he was one of the best rescue specialists, and as I watched him prepare his equipment, I came to the conclusion that he surely must know what he was doing."

What Friedli was doing was trying to solve the worst problem of a rescue on the north wall: anchoring the cables securely at the top. It was like trying to tie threads to the tipped edge of a cube of ice. There were a few stubby cornices, protrusions of rotten rock half-crumbled by thousands of years of weathering. But they were soft and porous, and pitons driven into them only split the rock and fell out, or mushed into the rock as though they were being driven into lard. The longest cable was only six hundred feet, at least 150 feet less than the distance down to the red tent in the exit cracks. And Friedli had to use up two hundred feet of the precious cable tying it around one of the cornices. The work took until three in the afternoon, but now someone could go down for a reconnaissance of the face. Seiler, Perrenoud and a handful of the other Swiss had arrived. Friedli asked for volunteers. Seiler, Perrenoud and Terray stepped forward. Friedli pointed to Seiler, and strapped him into a sling attached to the end of the cable. Visibility was excellent, and radio contact with the Kleine Scheidegg spotters below had improved. Friedli told them: "We are going to lower a man."

Belayed by the others, Seiler began to back down the mountain. He had to move with consummate care; the slightest disruption of the face might send tons of ice and snow cascading down on the very men they were trying to save. Soon he came to the lower edge of the summit snow field and dropped over the side into the nearly ninety-degree incline at the top of the exit cracks. Already the Scheidegg spotters were hurriedly radioing to Friedli that Seiler was coming down several hundred feet to the west of the red tent. But this was merely a reconnaissance mission, and Seiler went all the way to the end of his tether, four hundred feet down. Now he could see the red tent below him and, to his left a stiffening wind sending ripples across the plastic surface. There were no signs of life. He had hoped to find three climbers there—the ones who had gone ahead, leaving their comrade below on the ledge. For ten minutes, he shouted, but except for the wind, all was silence. Carefully noting the exact position of the tent, he gave the signal for the upward haul. Radio communications began to worsen again, and Seiler found himself wrenched upward when he did not want to be, and forced to stand for long periods on narrow ledges covered with ice and snow while he shouted to be pulled up. Soon he could not feel his toes; the stark chill of the wall had permeated his climbing boots. It was more than two hours before he reached the top again, frostbitten and bruised. He headed immediately down the west wall for medical assistance.

Now Friedli, taciturn as ever, ordered the tedious task of repositioning the anchoring two hundred feet to the west, nearer the spot where Terray had told him it should have been in the first place. More hours were consumed, and the summit ridge began to swarm with volunteers. Cassin, Mauri and Eiselin had arrived after the high-route Swiss; then came some of the Swiss who had been forced down from the Jungfraujoch; then the men of the Mountain Guard, and finally the Poles, bearing heavy loads of equipment on their backs. Just before nightfall, the new anchoring was ready, and Friedli announced that he would make a descent himself. It was seven-thirty in the evening; visibility was still good, and Friedli could hear the Scheidegg spotters and the men on the summit loud and clear in his helmet earphones. The Scheidegg reported that the single man on the lower edge was moving around, flapping his arms to keep warm. But nothing was happening at the red tent. Either the three other climbers were huddled inside, or they were dead.

Friedli backed down the summit snow field and dropped over the edge toward the point where the Scheidegg told him the tent bivouac could be spotted. Dangling slowly downward, his face lashed by ice crystals blown off the wall by the accelerating winds, he reached a point several hundred feet above the White Spider. But he was even then too far to the west; with disgust, he realized that the anchorings above would have to be changed again. Just before giving the order to haul him up, Friedli shouted down the face, and back came a voice saying something Friedli could not understand. Now he knew that at least one man was still alive on the wall. He was lifted back to the top at eight-fifteen, in time to see the men of the mountain Guard of Munich, equally confident of their own experience and ability, digging out a work platform precisely over the fall line to the red tent. Off to one side, driving pitons into a rock cornice and installing pulley and brake equipment, was the one-eyed Gramminger. Rolls of steel cable, a quarter of an inch thick but capable of supporting a weight of almost two tons, had arrived.

Friedli climbed out of his harness and radioed the Scheidegg that he felt optimistic; he knew there was life on the wind-swept face, and he told them he would make a final attempt to reach the stranded men by moonlight. The last rays of the sun slid behind the summit of the Mönch, and reporters at the Scheidegg telescope prepared to keep an all-night vigil and flash the news of rescue to their newspapers.

But nothing ever came that easily on the Eiger. Soon a sharp, cold wind hit the summit; the temperature began dropping until it reached a little above zero, and there were freeze-up problems with the equipment. Friedli radioed the Scheidegg that they would have to halt operations for the night and seek shelter themselves. Von Almen, on the radio below, signed off, and promised to resume the watch at dawn.

While the rescuers were scraping their sleeping quarters out of the icy overhang on the ridge, a final volunteer clambered up on the ridge. It was Walter Seeger, the young architect of Pfullingen and close friend and ropemate of Günther Nothdurft. His odyssey to the summit of the Eiger had been almost a miniature summation of the experiences of all the others. That afternoon in Zürich, he had heard about the rescuers on the radio. He had borrowed a motorbike and raced to Grindelwald, where he called on Willi Balmer and received the same hopeless message as all the rest. Not knowing the way to the summit, he borrowed crampons, walked up the railroad tracks to the Eigergletscher Hotel, and then forced the west wall alone as night fell. Now, having climbed ten thousand feet in a single day, he announced that he was ready to assist. His arrival brought the number of rescuers to fifty. It would not be even one too many.

CHAPTER ELEVEN

Slowly, very slowly, as he sat on the little ledge Friday, reason had returned to Claudio Corti. He did not know how long he had been sitting, but it was still daylight, perhaps late in the afternoon, to judge by the sun which had now dropped down the back of the mountain. His head ached dully; he reached up and touched a muslin bandage which swathed it. As he made this motion, he felt a pain in his hands; he pulled off his gloves and saw the long, bloody serrations in his palms. And then he remembered. Stefano, poor Stefano, was on another ledge down the mountain. And the Germans? Where were they? Painfully, he turned his head and looked up the exit cracks where he had seen them a few hours before, smiling wanly down at him. A light rain was falling, and the crack disappeared in the mists. They must be beating their way to the top. They would send help, and he and Stefano would be saved.

He looked over his perch, and saw that it was almost the same as Stefano's: a yard or so wide, four or five feet long. But it was more sheltered than the other, if any place on this mountain could be described as sheltered. The ledge was indented in the mountain, back from the wall, and protected at one end by a shattered pillar covered with rock rubble. At least he would not be troubled with avalanche and rockfall. He saw them now and then in the rain; they would roar down the mountain and arc out over his head. He shuddered for Stefano below.

When the clouds parted, he could see the Kleine Schei-degg hotels and once he caught a glimpse of Grindelwald and the little meadow-village of Alpiglen. But he could not see down to Stefano; bulging shields of rock cut off the view. And he could see neither to right nor left across the precipice. The ridges which marked the east and west edges of the north face were shut off to him by the pillar on one side and the wall on the other. He felt a complete isolation.

"Stefano!" he called down the face. "Stefano!" But there was no answer. He spotted the rucksack left by the Germans. There was no food inside; all of their food had long since been roped down to Longhi. But inside the rucksack was the red plastic tent. Moving slowly on the ledge, he pitched it and secured it firmly to the wall with an ice hammer and a few pitons the Germans had left him. Then he crawled inside. His clothes were drenched through, but at least he would get no wetter. He took off the red wool shirt which clung stickily to his skin, put his jacket back on, and gingerly adjusted the skiing hat and wool hood over the muslin of his bandage. Hardly had he finished the simple but laborious task of rearranging his clothing when a metallic drone came to his ears. He groped his way out of the tent and saw an airplane buzzing the face, not more than two hundred feet away. He waved the shirt with all his strength, and shouted, "Help! Help me!" But the plane moved off into the clouds. He did not know whether the pilot had spotted him in his depressed bivouac.

He could feel the blood from his head wound dripping down over his face. He removed the bandage, picked up a handful of snow and packed it on the gash to relieve the hemorrhaging. And then it was night.

Sitting inside the tent, he began to feel cold; the winds and rain were getting worse, and lightning was crackling around the face. He kept himself sternly immobile to keep

the lightning from finding him. Through the long hours
of the storm, he sat rigidly, afraid to move. Then the
lightning stopped; the rain changed to snow, and finally
stopped altogether. But the winds whined more violently
than ever, and he could feel the temperature dropping hour
by hour. He tried to move his fingers and his toes and
found he could not. Pounding his hands against the ice for
several hours, he brought the circulation back to his fingers.
Painstakingly, he took off his climbing boots to massage his
feet and ankles; the cold was so intense that he felt a
humming in his wound, under the muslin and the ski cap
and the hood. He became aware of a terrible thirst. He
knew that eating ice was an act of desperation on a mountain. Ice was devoid of minerals; it merely chilled the
stomach and carried off the minerals already in the body.
Sometimes it was contaminated with glacier dust, and this
could tie knots in a man's stomach. Still he shoved handfuls
of ice into his mouth, breaking his teeth against it, until
the area around him in the tent had been scraped down to
bare rock. He wanted to sleep, but, in his delirium, he said
to himself that the cold water inside him would freeze, and
he would die slowly, freezing from the inside out. He rubbed
snow across his face every five or ten minutes; the air was
so cold, and his face was so chilled, that the snow felt
warm and comforting, and the simple task of applying it
kept him awake for many hours. But then he dozed off,
sheltered by the red tent, and dreamed that he was a child
again, lying in his mother's arms in Olginate.

When he awoke, it was already late in the morning. A
red glow suffused the roof of the tent; the sun must be
shining. For a long time, he rubbed his arms and legs to
restore the circulation. He did a sort of cramped calisthenics
on the ledge, sliding his legs back and forth until they began
to feel warmer. He washed his face with snow, and crawled

out of the tent. There was the sun, big and warming; he laid his red wool shirt on the tent to dry, and then he heard the airplane again. This time the sky was clear, and he could make out two figures in the plane as it flitted past his ledge. He waved the red shirt again, and shouted, "Here! Here! Help me!" He was sure that they had seen him, but in his jumbled state of mind, he felt annoyed that they had merely flown away. A few minutes later more planes came by, crossing and recrossing the face. He could see the pilots looking in his direction, and he cried with all his strength, "Here! Here! Can't you see me?" Then he became enraged and cursed the pilots for leaving him all alone. "Fools!" he shouted. "Idiots! Why do you not come for me?" They were so close; his life was being taken from him, and those stupid fliers were doing nothing about it. Below he could see Grindelwald, the Kleine Scheidegg, the miniature tracks of the Jungfraujoch Railway. It seemed he could reach out and touch them all. People were living and walking around down there. Could they not see that his life was being taken away?

The planes came by all day long, and soon he merely sat and watched them, no longer flapping the red shirt, no longer calling or even acknowledging their waves. Darkness was coming on; the lights began to twinkle from the valleys below. When the last flicker of daylight passed, he looked down into the valley and said aloud: "They don't come any more." He pronounced his last good-byes to everybody: to his mother and father, to Fulvia Losa, to Zucchi and Bigio and all his old comrades, and to poor Stefano, trapped down below. "I do not see them again," he said. "Not even once again." He rapped his ice hammer against the wall and shook loose some chips. Piece by piece he took the bits of ice into the tent and made a mound of them. Then he slowly pulled the tent-flap closed and lay down with his head on the ice. "Now," he said, "this is my tomb." He could feel his heartbeat only faintly; his breathing was slow and irregular. His body was numbed with fatigue and cold, and life seemed so far away that it was as if he had never lived at all. He closed his eyes and said in a low voice: "*Muoio qui.* I die here."

CHAPTER TWELVE

Even under ideal conditions, the summit ridge of the Eiger was no place for a bivouac. It sliced into the sky almost like a giant ax-blade, tilted slightly downward from west to east. It was possible to walk for several hundred yards along the ridge with one foot stepping on the north wall and the other on the south; it was also possible to misstep and fall all the way down either wall. To worsen matters, the whole ridge was covered by an ill-fitting icecap of varying thickness. In places, snow and ice had slid out from underneath, cutting away the underpinning fixing the cap to the ridge. A few raps of the ice ax over spots like these and the climber would plummet through to his death. It was all but impossible to tell the good surface from the bad; one hacked away and hoped for the best.

As darkness fell on the ridge that Saturday night, and fifty climbers from six nations laid their plans in a farrago of tongues and accents, it was decided to remain overnight on the mountaintop despite the dangers. Work must resume promptly at dawn; already the men trapped below had endured seven or eight enervating bivouacs on the face, more than anyone in Eiger's macabre history. They must be saved —if, indeed, they still survived—with no more delay than absolutely necessary. Some few rescuers made the decision to go back down the west flank for a night's sleep in the Eigergletscher Hotel, and to return in the morning; but most of them stayed and began hacking caverns into the treacherous icecap. The unimpeded winds from the north swirled the chips of ice back into their faces as they dug carefully, probing for thin spots and making sure they did not cut an inch deeper than they had to.

After a few hours, all the rescuers were encamped in their recessed igloos for the night. Those who spoke Latin tongues stayed together in one hole; the Swiss split into a few groups; Gramminger dug a one-man shelter for himself and his equipment, and the other members of the Mountain Guard lay close together for warmth, thirty feet away. The Poles were the best off; they had brought complete bivouac equipment and at least enough food to make a meal. For the rest, there was almost nothing to eat or drink. Terray and de Booy, sheltered now with Eiselin, Cassin, and Mauri, had blitzed up the west wall without even eating breakfast. The other three had nothing. They had not expected an overnight bivouac on this chill summit.

Huddled together, the five men carried on their conversations with difficulty. Terray could speak French, English and Spanish; so he could communicate with Eiselin, who spoke French, English, German and a little Italian, and with Mauri, who spoke Italian and Spanish. Mauri would pass the conversation along to Cassin, who spoke only Italian. The polyglot de Booy, who understood all the languages ricocheting about the bivouac, acted as a sort of senior interpreter for the group. On the whole, it seemed to Terray, he had seen many worse bivouacs, and many with less of an atmosphere of fellowship. Eiselin proved to be an amiable young man; Cassin and Mauri were experienced Alpinists who knew how to live with the situation, and de Booy, the companionable teacher from Amsterdam, brought a glow of warmth and solidarity to the group.

Further down the icecap, the Germans were having a less satisfactory time of it. Gramminger had intended to buy food in Grindelwald, but they had entrained for the summit before the first stores opened up in the morning. He had brought a little salami and bread from Munich, barely enough to provide a few snacks on the drive to the Ober-land, but it was impossible to eat the leftover food without something to drink. His Mountain Guard comrades had a gasoline cooker with which to thaw snow for tea, but in the confusion at the Grindelwald station in the morning, the Poles had promised to bring extra fuel for the cooker, and then had forgotten. Now they were limited to the few drops in the tank of the cooker, barely enough to start the device, but certainly not enough to melt snow to provide liquid for any substantial number of men.

"Well," Gramminger said to himself as he snuggled into his ice-walled lodging for the night, "I shall not have my evening cup of tea after all." He pulled the heavy bivouac sacks over himself, arranged the pieces of the stripped-down winch, which the heat of his body would keep thawed through the night, and prepared to sleep. He had not yet begun to doze, his head swarming with the logistic problems of the day to come, when he saw a familiar face peering owlishly into his cavern. "Yes, Alfred," said Gramminger. "What is it that has taken you out of your shelter on such a night?"

"It is like this, Wiggerl," the burly Hellepart said against the moaning of the wind. "We are together in a nice hole, and we even have a candle for light and a little warmth for our hands. But we do not have an extra bivouac sack to cover over the entrance to the hole, and the wind keeps blowing our candle out. We thought perhaps—"

"I will strike you a trade, Alfred. You have the spirit cooker?"

"Yes, but there are only a few drops of fuel left in it."

"If there are a few drops of fuel left, you can brew me some tea. And if the tea is enjoyable, I will give you an extra bivouac sack."

It was an odd bargain, Hellepart thought as he struggled

back to his cavern. But it would be worth a try. He fired up the cooker and began thawing some snow. The fuel sputtered and fumed and produced mostly smoke, and while a few crystals of unmelted snow still swirled around in the cup, the flame went out altogether. Hellepart dropped a tea bag in the chilly mixture and kneaded it until the water took on a vaguely rusty color. "It is tea," Hellepart told his comrades. "But is it *enjoyable* tea?" He carried the cup of liquid back to Gramminger's hole and passed it inside with a grandiose gesture. "Here," said Hellepart. "We have lived up to our part of the bargain."

There was a long silence from within, and then a bivouac sack came hurtling out at Hellepart's feet. "You do not brew a very good tea, Alfred," the leader's voice came from inside. "But I would have given you the sack anyway."

"I always knew that, Wiggerl," Hellepart answered. He went back to the others and rigged the extra sack over the hole to shut out the wind. The men of the Mountain Guard went slowly off to sleep.

At dawn the icy Tower of Babel on top of the Eiger summit sprang quickly to life. Gramminger was first up, and began the complex operation of laying out the cable system for new descents. The main problem was to anchor the large, drum-type winch on the shifting icecap. He made it fast with ice-pitons, then tied it to the porous rock of the cornice with several other cables. Another cable was wound around a big block of ice and connected to the winch, and several loose ropes were added on; as a final safety measure, some of the rescuers would grip these ropes tightly, scratch secure stances into the ice with their crampons, and hold on. Gramminger stepped back and surveyed his work. It was an insecure arrangement; he would have given anything for one solid outcropping of firm rock as a cornerstone for the rig. But the top of this mountain offered no concessions to the mechanical needs of the rescue party. They would have to make do.

Friedli watched the Germans set up their equipment and recognized that they were doing a skilled job under the adverse conditions. Still, he was not going to abdicate his own responsibilities in the operation. For all his deep respect for Gramminger and the Mountain Guard, he had serious misgivings about the winch. Under stress, it might tear loose and hurtle down the cliff, impartially taking rescuers and rescued to their deaths below. And even if the winch remained in place, he doubted that it was geared low enough to enable its operators to haul up the men below. At best, it would be an inch-by-inch struggle, taking long hours. And at this stage of the rescue, the life expectancies of the four men down below had to be measured in minutes.

Weighing all these factors, the skilled technician of Thun ordered a backstopping operation of his own. While Gramminger and the Mountain Guard struggled to anchor the winch, Friedli called together a work gang of Swiss and ordered them to extend the length of the level path which had been cut parallel to the ridge on the south side of the peak. Soon Friedli's men had hacked a path almost two hundred feet long, and had even rigged a sort of rope fence on its outer edge. Now men could walk along the trench in comparative safety. If the winch failed to work, the cable could be passed through pulleys over the top and back to crews in the trench, and old-fashioned, dependable manpower could take over the pulling operation. Friedli's move, taken with his usual taciturnity and strictly on the basis of his own forebodings, was a brilliant stroke of planning, even though it seemed to the digging crews in the trench that their leader had simply found a way to keep them busy and uncomfortable.

Overnight, the master plan for this Sunday morning had been worked out. It was known that Longhi was alone on a ledge about one thousand feet down, and it was assumed that the other three were in the tent several hundred feet above Longhi's perch. Reconnaissance pilots, toward the end of Saturday, had noticed Longhi slumping on his ledge. Probably he was in the worst condition of the four. Therefore the tentative plan was to lower a man past the red tent and down to Longhi, give him first aid and a stimulant, and haul him up to the tent. Then other rescuers would go down on the cable and bring the four men, one by one, to safety on the ridge. The only remaining question was whom to send down on the first trip. An Italian-speaking rescuer would have good verbal communication with Longhi and his comrade. But he would not be able to talk to the Germans. A German-speaking rescuer would have the opposite problem. Gramminger and Friedli talked the situation over, and the deciding factor was that the Italian members of the rescue party had had no experience with the Gramminger equipment, but the men of the Mountain Guard knew their gear like firemen. Gramminger and Friedli selected Alfred Hellepart, an old hand at mountain rescues, and a man of tremendous strength and courage. At two hundred pounds, he was the heaviest of the Mountain Guard crew, but the quarter-inch cable had a tensile strength of nearly two tons, and Hellepart's bull-like power would be needed below. Gramminger fixed his friend to the end of the cable, strapped on the short-wave radio, covered Hellepart's head with a white plastic helmet, attached a rucksack to his back, and sent him over the side. Friedli took over the radio for the over-all direction of the operation, and Gramminger scurried to the anchorage of the winch, there to stand ultimate guard over the life of his friend in case the equipment began to rip loose. Despite the insecurity of the anchorage, Gramminger felt fairly confident that it would stay in place. And if it did not, the other members of the rescue team would hold tightly, and somehow they would work

Hellepart back up to the top. They had had to improvise before, and they had never lost a man. Neither, however, had they attempted a rescue one thousand feet down, or from such a treacherous perch. "Well," Gramminger said to himself, "we shall merely do our best." What worried him most was the weather. In good weather, the Mountain Guard could accomplish almost anything. But on this unprotected summit, the slightest break in the weather could mean the end of the whole operation. Even a minor electrical storm could be fatal; the steel cable was also a long lightning rod, and the man dangling at its end would risk electrocution. If clouds came, the important radio liaison with the spotters below at the Kleine Scheidegg would be useless, and the descents would have to be made on a hit-or-miss basis. And if there were high winds, the rescuers would be in danger of losing their delicate stances on the knife-edge of the summit. The weather simply had to remain clear. But a glance at the sky gave Gramminger a chill of apprehension. The sun hung between bilious clouds in a dirty-gray rectangle of visibility. To Gramminger, it seemed a poisonous yellow, a certain harbinger of storm. High black clouds could be seen coming down from the north. He was sure that they would reach the Eiger within hours and begin to discharge their loads of snow and rain and electricity against the face. If they did, the rescuers would have no choice but to beat a hurried retreat down the west flank. There could be no question of risking dozens of lives by trying to remain on the summit during a storm.

CHAPTER THIRTEEN

It was exactly eight o'clock on Sunday morning when Alfred Hellepart began moving down the mountain into aloneness. As he walked slowly backward on the fifty-degree angle of the summit ice field, watching his friends operate the winch above him, he set about preparing himself psychologically. From long experience, he knew that one had to purge one's mind of all outside thoughts; the entire concentration had to be on the job at hand, and on the men to be rescued. One could not think at all of oneself; the slightest glimmer of fear could be deadly. Nor could he allow his thoughts to drift back to Munich, to his wife and his eleven-year-old son. From this minute on, they must be forgotten, until he had succeeded or failed in his rescue mission.

Certainly, there was no need to worry about the cable. The experienced Gramminger was up at the anchorage, protecting him as he had so many times before. The men of the Mountain Guard had an almost childlike faith in their leader; they acted on his orders without question or hesitation. In practice exercises, Hellepart had carried two men on his back up the side of a mountain, and the cable had held. He would press a button in his mind and give the matter no further thought.

Now he was halfway down the summit ice field, and he tested the portable radio. The contact was excellent; he could hear Friedli loud and clear, and Friedli could hear him. When he had gone 250 feet, almost to the end of the field, he heard Friedli telling him to make himself secure on his crampons; the cable had to be disconnected from the winch and joined to the next three-hundred-foot length by a frog coupling. Hellepart waited until the go-ahead came from the top, backed over the last few feet of the snow field, and found himself looking down the vast sweep of the north wall. For a moment, despite all his psychological preparations, he felt wild panic. An indescribable feeling of abandonment came over him; he could no longer see the men on the top, and instinctively he looked up at the quarter-inch cable spinning up into the mists, like a thin strand of cotton thread. Below him the north wall fell endlessly away, down and down and down, black and menacing, broken only by a few insignificant snow ledges. Dangling from the cable, he gulped for air, and almost forgot what he had come for. Just then the voice of Gramminger broke in on the radio. "You are doing fine, Alfred," the calm voice said. "Everything is secure for you. Keep control of yourself, and remember that there are men on the wall depending on you for their lives." The soothing words brought composure back to Hellepart; he was no longer alone; he felt the strong ties to the men above, all their concentration fixed on him and his task, and he gave the order to continue letting the cable down. Off to his right, he could see a black rift coming up, one of the gaping exit cracks leading to the White Spider. He made a short traverse to the crack, and began wriggling his way obliquely downward. He did not know if this was the right route, but at the moment it was the only one. Two thousand feet below him, he could see the morning mists walking up the wall. For brief seconds, he glimpsed the village of Alpiglen, but then the mists closed together again and blanketed the valley. All around him the wind probed the holes and cracks on the mountain, and the low, hollow "whoo" gave him an uncomfortable feeling.

Now he had to find a secure stance again, to hold himself against the wall while another three-hundred-foot roll of cable was attached above. Friedli's voice crackled down to him from above: "All is well. You will be on your way in a few minutes." The signal came, and he continued his descent. After a hundred more feet, he went on the air to tell Friedli that he was coming in sight of the Spider. Against the low howl of the wind, he talked to the summit, and during that brief conversation he heard another human voice, barely audible at first, then growing louder and coming from the east. He traversed toward the voice and came to a shattered pillar bulging out across the face. He stepped onto the pillar and sent rocks and rubble clattering down the face with his crampons. Still he went on, only partially supported by the cable which now had assumed a sort of J-shape as it followed him on the level course across the pillar. About sixty feet away, he spotted a man in a half-sitting, half-lying position on a narrow ledge pitched with a small red tent. Nervously, he pushed the transmitting button and signaled the summit: "I have found a man."

Across the litter-covered pillar, Hellepart shouted: "Who are you? Are you Mayer, or Nothdurft?" The voice came back: "*Italiano.*"

Slowly, still sending tons of rubble down the mountain, Hellepart continued the difficult traverse. Now he was within six or seven feet of the Italian, and he could hear the man calling, "*Mangiare!* Something to eat!" Hellepart fumbled in his pocket, found a frozen half-bar of black, hard Cailler chocolate, and tossed it across the edge to the hungry man. The Italian did not even pause to remove the wrapper. He rammed the chocolate into his mouth and began to chew. His mouth full of paper and chocolate, the man called to Hellepart: "*Sigaretta?*" But Hellepart had none. He paused for a moment and considered the situation. He could traverse the remaining few feet of the pillar, but only at increasing risk to himself, since he no longer dangled straight down from the cable. And if he reached the Italian in this manner, he would be unable to make the rescue. The two men, no matter what their condition, could not have effected the traverse back across the rubble without undue danger. Hellepart decided to retreat to the exit crack and ask the summit to pull him up to another position. From there he would try to make a straight perpendicular descent to the Italian. "Take me up," Hellepart called to the summit. "I am going to look for another route." A hard jerk on the cable yanked him off the pillar and out into space. Spinning in mid-air, he fought to turn himself toward the wall so that he could take up the shock of the return impact with his legs. He had barely succeeded in twisting around when he crashed into the wall feet first. "All right," said Hellepart to the summit, "haul me straight up. I will tell you when to stop."

Up he went, inches at a time, for 150 feet, and then set himself into a slow swing until he was able to grab a jutting rock straight above the Italian. "Now let me down," he instructed. As he descended a sheer gully, stones began to shake loose again, and he shouted to the Italian to take cover. Finally he dropped the last few feet and onto the ledge. While the marooned man mumbled *"Grazie! Grazie!"* and put his arms around Hellepart, the German called triumphantly to the summit: "I am with the Italian!" It was nine-fifteen, and he had been on the wall for more than an hour. The Italian gave his name, and Hellepart reported it to the summit. Friedli asked where the others were. Hellepart said to Corti: "Where is Longhi? Where is Mayer? Where is Nothdurft?"

Corti pointed down the mountain. The two men leaned over the edge and called, but there was no response. Hellepart asked Corti in German, "Your condition?" Corti understood—the phrase is similar in both languages—and answered, *"Buona."* But Hellepart, seeing that the man's knees were trembling, ordered him to sit down, and gave him coffee from a thermos which had been provided by the

Poles. Corti was talking in Italian, and Hellepart got the impression from the torrent of words in the peculiar dialect that Nothdurft and Mayer had tried to force through to the top and that Corti had not seen them for several days. He looked at Corti's scarred hand and his bloodied head and decided that the Italian's condition was too poor to permit him to attempt a climb up to the top on a separate cable. Hellepart would have to make the carry on his back. He radioed to the summit for an Italian-speaking man to take the radio and explain the situation to Corti. Cassin's voice came on, and Hellepart handed the speaking mechanism to Corti, who seemed befuddled by it and nervously pushed the wrong buttons. Finally the contact was established, and Cassin could talk to his friend from the Ragni. "*Rispondi,* Claudio," Cassin's voice said. "This is Cassin. Now listen to me: you have not the strength to go up by yourself. Watch how he shows you how to get up on his shoulders! Try everything to make it easy for your rescuer! Drink something when he gives you to drink. Remember, you are safe. Do not lose your spirit!" Hellepart took back the radio as the last words of Cassin crackled through the earphones: "*Coraggio,* Claudio, *coraggio!*"

Hellepart took a final look at Corti's tiny resting place. It was totally cleared of ice and snow, gobbled up by Corti in his terrible hunger and thirst. Some of his teeth were broken and splintered, shattered against the hard, cold ice for a last few useless "meals." Hellepart packed the rucksack, strapped it on the sitting Corti's back, and began lacing him into the webbing of a Gramminger-Sitz. He sat down with his back to Corti's front and pulled the harnesses of the human back-pack around his own chest and up over his shoulders. This left no place for the radio; using snap links to lengthen the girth, he fixed the apparatus so that it dangled across his chest. Bearing the uncomfortable weight, he struggled to his feet and snapped the cable in place. All these preparations had taken nearly an hour. "We are ready," he said to the summit. It was ten o'clock.

Back came Friedli's voice: "We have been rearranging the equipment. It will take us a few minutes more."

Hellepart sat down with his heavy load and waited for the signal. Finally it came. "We bring you up now," Friedli called. "Prepare yourself!"

Hellepart wrenched himself into a standing position, but still the cable hung slack above him. "What is the matter?" he called to the summit.

"We are having a little trouble," Friedli answered. Long minutes went by, and then the cable began to tense. Hellepart pressed his feet against the wall and pushed outward with all his strength so that he would keep the cable from rubbing against the wall and prevent it from fouling. Now the wind began to hum across the tightening thread of steel. It sounded to Hellepart like a giant violin string, starting on a low note and gradually whining higher as it tensed, until it had reached a screaming, piercing pitch. And still they did not move up from the ledge. He looked above him at the delicate strand and wondered, for the first time, if it would hold.

On top, Friedli's fears about the winch had only increased as it had become necessary to haul Hellepart back up 150 feet to find a better route down to the Italian. By now there were eight hundred feet of cable reaching down the mountain. Where it made contact with the rock, it had abraded fissures of its own, increasing the friction and multiplying the force required for the upward pull. The men cranking the winch had barely been able to lift Hellepart up to his new stance, and after lowering him back down to the ledge, Friedli discussed the situation with Gramminger. "I do not think we can use the winch to pull the weight of two men," Friedli said. Gramminger agreed. While Hellepart went about his tedious task of readying Corti for the ascent, the crew on top discarded the winch and prepared to shift over to raw manpower. It was a quick improvisation, made possible only by Friedli's foresight in ordering the pulling path dug into the south ridge. Now the cable would go up to the ridge and through a direction-changing roller placed on top of the rotten cornice. The roller would steer the cable back along the path, where thirty men were scrambling into position. At intervals of twenty feet, pulling ropes were attached to the cable by clamps which could be loosened and moved along to a new position.

Now teams of five were in place at each pulling rope, waiting for the signal from Friedli to begin the haul. A last-minute check was made of the three security brakes on the cable; they were so constructed that the cable could be pulled upward through them, but at the slightest accidental downward movement they would clamp tightly shut. As a final security, Gramminger remained at the big block of ice on the far end of the pulling path to anchor each new length of slack cable to the block as it was hauled in. Now they were ready.

With the voice of a Swiss drill sergeant, Friedli shouted to the men to haul away. They strained backward against the pulling ropes. But nothing moved. More hands were added to the ropes, and the order was repeated. Still the cable did not budge. Fearful that the combined strength of all the rescuers would snap the tensing lifeline to the two men below, Friedli frantically waved the operation to a halt. He did not think it possible that the cable had become wedged into the rock below; the soft limestone on the upper part of the Eiger might increase the friction, but it would not have been solid enough to imprison the cable against all this pressure. He decided that the mechanical equipment must have jammed. If his diagnosis was incorrect, if indeed the cable *was* fouled tightly on the mountain, they would have

to abandon Corti and try to find some way to bring Hellepart back up. Nervously, Friedli went from device to device
and finally came to one which had fouled. He cleared the
jam and ordered the crews to begin pulling again. The
cable tensed and whined in the wind, after a few long
seconds, the men could feel it begin to move.

Now, at last, the long violin string had hit a pitch and
held it, and Hellepart was coming up the mountain, his
human cargo heavy on his back, the radio dangling clumsily
in front of him. At first, the ascent was not on a true perpendicular line. They swayed from side to side as the cable
whipped them about; Hellepart shoved his crampons into
the icy patina on the wall, seeking to steady himself, and
sent slabs of ice and rock crashing down the wall. Every
fifty feet, he had to cling to the wall, leaning as far forward
as he could, while the men on the summit secured the cable
and moved up to new pulling positions. These were agonizing delays to the strong man of Munich; sometimes he
would have to kneel against a tiny ledge, gripping an outcropping of rock with his knees the way a jockey grips a
horse, the harsh metal edges of the radio digging into his
chest. Sometimes he had to stand upright on scallops of
snow, with all the weight of Corti on his shoulders. Once
he said aloud, in a slightly annoyed, slightly quizzical voice:
"Well, he's quite heavy, this fellow." But Corti seemed not
to have heard. He was mumbling, *Fame! Fame!* and
whenever Hellepart kneeled against the wall, Corti would
push his own face into the snow and bite off big mouthfuls.
   "Don't gobble so much snow!" Hellepart hollered. "It
is bad for the stomach." But the famished Corti took his
cold snacks anyway.
   After about forty minutes of the torturous rise, the cable
rasped over the last foot of the exit cracks and swung the
two men onto the summit ice field. Out of the shadow of the

overhang, they now could feel the rays of the sun, and Corti reacted peculiarly. *"Que bello e il sole,"* he said in a strangely loud voice. "How beautiful the sun is." Then he slumped forward into a coma. Hellepart recognized this as a shock reaction, and he knew that men in a seriously weakened condition could die from it. He would have to force the final 250 feet of the field. Up he came, staggering like a drunk under his heavy load, while Friedli shouted encouragement from the top. Now Hellepart was taking almost all of Corti's weight, receiving little assistance from the cable which no longer hung straight down to hold them in firm suspension. The men on top knew he was forcing, and increased their own pace, once pulling too far too fast and nearly wrenching Hellepart and Corti face forward into the wet snow of the ice field. Hellepart merely regained his balance, kicked up through the sticky snow, and finally, fifty-nine minutes after the ascent had begun, stumbled with his cargo across the ridge. "Help me out of this!" he shouted to Friedli and pitched forward into the snow. Gasping for breath, while the others wrenched at the harnesses holding Corti and the radio to him, Hellepart felt a slap on the shoulder and heard an unfamiliar voice say, "Good! You have done well!" Relieved of his load, he was lifted to his feet and congratulated all around. "A cigarette!" he said. "I would like a cigarette!" Weak, and afraid he would slip off the summit, he wobbled to the safety of a bivouac hole for a smoke and a rest.

CHAPTER FOURTEEN

Lying in the snow on the lip of the summit ice field, Claudio Corti looked, to the rescuers who swarmed around him, like a live corpse. His eyesockets, shadowed by the hood around his head, were deep-sunken and black, almost like those of a skull which had sat for decades on somebody's mantelpiece. His skin hung loosely against his face; it was apparent that he had lost a critical amount of his body weight. *"Carne,"* he mumbled. "Meat." The Polish doctor, Jerzy Hajdukiewicz, pushed through the onlookers and injected a stimulant into Corti's arm. Someone passed a glass of tea laced with cognac; Corti took it in one gulp. Hajdukiewicz ordered a removal to a safer position. Two strong Poles lifted the patient to his feet and hustled him off to one side. Wrapped in blankets and placed in an ice hut, he seemed hardly to understand what had happened. But as the stimulant began to take effect, he suddenly became manic. To Mauri, he said: "Well, now that I know the route up here, will you come with me to climb it?" Hellepart appeared at the edge of the huddled group; Corti saw him and called, *"Grazie! Grazie!"* in an ebullient, festive manner, as though everything was now a total success, as though no other lives remained in danger now that his own was saved. Then he turned quickly to Mauri and blurted out: "This time the wall caught me, but next time I will catch the wall!"

Terray, Seeger and Cassin grouped tightly around to find out what had happened on the wall and to seek clues to the whereabouts of the others. Corti turned confidently to Cassin and muttered, "Riccardo, do you think they will write that I was the first Italian to climb the north wall?"

"How can they write that?" Cassin answered. "Can't you see how you got up here, on the back of another man?" Corti looked perplexed. Seeger, the close friend of Nothdurft, reddened and said to a comrade: "It is like taking a fist in the face to hear him talk like that."

Several minutes went by before Corti could be brought through his state of shock and questioned seriously. Out of a maze of contradictions and incoherencies, the rescuers learned that he had not seen the Germans since Friday afternoon, but that he assumed they were clinging to a bivouac positioned somewhere up the exit cracks. Longhi, he told them, was well down the mountain, but at least three hundred feet further to the east. This jibed with information being radioed up from the Scheidegg, and now the rescuers knew they would have to begin all over again the arduous job of repositioning the equipment. While a crew went off to prepare a new anchorage, Friedli ordered one more descent down the same route taken by Hellepart so that the whole radiator grill of the exit cracks could be studied for signs of the Germans. Hellepart was exhausted, and Friedli turned to the most skilled climber in the group. "Terray," he said, "do you still volunteer to go down?"

"Of course," the Frenchman answered.

Terray was buttoned into the harness, and a radio was strapped to his chest. Hajdukiewicz gave him last-minute instructions on how to administer injections, and at 12:20 P.M., he went over the side. The sun shone brightly overhead; the black clouds to the north still hung high, but had moved much closer to the Oberland. A thick blanket of fog was creeping up the wall and already obscured the lower half. "We will have to hurry," Friedli called down. "The storm is on its way."

After the first stop for a new length of cable, Terray slid over the last few feet of the summit snow field and across a fringe of rocks marking the beginning of the exit cracks. He could see fresh scars in the soft limestone, where the cable carrying Hellepart and Corti had ground its own grooves into the ugly face. Ten years had passed since Terray had been on this forbidding wall with his friend and fellow Chamonix guide Louis Lachenal, and it seemed to him, as he slipped smoothly down the exit cracks, that Lachenal was with him again, the same impish little balding man who had made the final sprint to the top of Annapurna with Maurice Herzog while Terray waited a few thousand feet below to help them both on the harrowing descent. Terray felt himself deeply moved as he saw that conditions on the north wall were almost the same as ten years before: the snow, the ice, the black rocks, all were unchanged. Even the heavy clouds darkening the sky, and the billows of mist coming up from the valley, were patterned as they had been then, just before an awful storm had almost swept the two climbers from the face. In his mind's eye he could see the supple Lachenal hauling himself over the last part of the exit cracks, standing finally at the base of the summit ice field and cracking to Terray as the two joined together: "Well, Guide, did this journey seem interesting to you?"

Now Lachenal was gone, victim two years before of a concealed crevasse in the Mont Blanc. Terray took a last look at the very spot where he had placed his liberating piton, the one which had taken him and Lachenal out of the exit cracks, and forced his concentration back on the lives and sufferings of two Germans and an Italian he had never seen. His eyes scanned the jagged cuts and ice shields on the upper face, but he could not make out the slightest sign of life. Was it possible for the Germans to be alive this far up? Terray doubted it. Unless they had somehow made their way off the face that Friday afternoon when Corti saw them last, they had had to bivouac for two freezing nights in the cracks, standing in place, or hanging against their ropes attached to the wall. Corti had described their condition. It was possible that Mayer might have been strong enough for two such bivouacs, Terray thought. But for the other, it would have been almost out of the question. Still, he would fulfill his assignment of surveillance. He had not yet come to the end of the second three-hundred-foot section of cable when, abruptly, his descent was halted. He pressed his transmitting button and said, "What has happened?" There was no response. Instead, over the three-way hookup, he heard a conversation in German between the spotters at the Kleine Scheidegg and the men at the summit. After more silence, a voice came through his earphones: "Hello, Terray, can you hear us? Answer, please."

"I hear you perfectly," Terray said. "Why did you stop my descent?"

But the voice from the summit repeated: "Hello, Terray, can you hear me? Answer, please!"

Terray realized that they were not getting his signal; the batteries in his transmitter must have been deadened by the cold and all the long hours of use. The chattering came incessantly through his earphones, now in German, now in French. He punched the transmitting button, shook up the pack, flicked at the microphone with his glove, but nothing would make his voice carry to the summit. Dangling in a rope sling at the end of the cable, he was not uncomfortable, but he could see the relentless movement of the black clouds, now lower and closer than before. He thought of the problems involved in making a cable ascent without radio communication and in a heavy storm. From the looks of this tempest speeding toward the wall, it might even be impossible for the pulling crews to remain on the summit. The lives of all the men up there would have to take precedence over anyone hanging below. Terray hoped that they would realize what was happening and quickly haul him up. But the minutes extended into an hour, then two hours, as he waited and worried. To occupy himself, and to keep from thinking about his plight, he made a few swings to right and left, but the spikes of his crampons dislodged so much thundering rubble that he decided to stop. If there was anyone alive below, he did not want to knock them off the north wall with avalanches of his own making.

Over on the northeast ridge, he could dimly make out a rope of four climbers who did not appear to see him. He remembered that some members of Nothdurft's climbing club in Bavaria had arrived on the summit that morning and had gone off to search the far ridge for signs of the Germans, in the unlikely hope that they had escaped across the overhangs and made their way to safety. Light fluffs of snow were beginning to blow around him, and Terray shouted with all his strength at the climbers a few hundred yards away. To his surprise, there was a response, but from below. Far down on the face, watching the approach of this same storm, the dogged Longhi was clinging to life, crying out as he had for three days now: *"Venite! Venite!* Come! Come!"* But Terray knew that no help would come to the man below on this day. Already it was too late to begin a new descent in the face of the storm. Now the cries of Longhi were blocked out by a voice in his earphones: "Scheidegg speaking. Hello, Terray. Can you hear us?" A few minutes later, Terray felt the vibrato of the cable as tension came back to it, and then he was on his way to the top. It was a lurching, bruising, blind ascent through transient clouds of snow which bit into his face and winds which now had increased sharply as the first fringes of the storm front began to lick over the wall. When he finally reached the top and fell into the arms of his friend de Booy, it was three o'clock. He rested for a few minutes, and then looked up to see what to him was an inexplicable sight: Corti, four hours after he had been hauled off the face closer to death than life, was still lying in the same ice hut on the summit. "My God!" Terray said to de Booy. "The man cannot stand another bivouac on this mountain. Can they not see that?" No matter that some of the rescuers had been digging feverishly at the new site for the cable; no matter that Friedli and his crew had been having their hands full trying to pull Terray up. Corti had been forgotten in the stress of the moment, and to Terray the oversight seemed inexcusable. "Now," he said to himself, "I have had enough of the Germanic slowness pervading this whole operation." Still shaken up by his own experience on the face, and more than a bit exasperated at the sight of the unmoved Corti, he said to himself: "I will stir things up."

To Gramminger and Hellepart, busily pursuing their bold plan of making a new drop to Longhi, he said: "We have saved one man's life, but we must save it fully. He must be taken to safety before the storm comes! Another night on this mountain will certainly kill him." Terray proposed that the party be split in half: one group to remain on the summit on the one-in-a-thousand chance that the storm might hold off long enough for another descent, the other to convoy Corti down the west wall and out of danger. Friedli and Gramminger agreed. The Swiss team would stay behind and man the cables. The others—Terray, de Booy, Hajdukiewicz and his fellow Poles, Gramminger and the Mountain Guard, and Corti's friends, Cassin and Mauri—would take over the dangerous descent to the Eigergletscher in the darkening afternoon. Once down, they would regroup later on the summit for further rescue attempts in the morning.

Terray lifted the inert Corti to his back and carried him five hundred feet along the well-worn edge of the summit ridge to the uppermost cornice of the Eiger. There, in a narrow pass leading through the rocks to the route down the west flank, he deposited the Italian on the snow, rolled him in several bivouac sacks, and installed him on a sort of half-sled half-stretcher. Using the long nylon ropes of the well-equipped Poles, the rescuers began to lower the half-conscious man. Every 120 feet, they had to halt to drive new pitons into the rocks and belay the operation's next step. Now a sleety rain was beginning to fall; quickly it covered the rock with a slippery coating. Pitoning became difficult; Terray had to scrape the slush away to find rock for the anchorings. The whole group was still on the most dangerous part of the west wall: the sharply-angled pitch leading down from the peak. Darkness was coming, and the edge of the storm was ripping and shoving at the precariously fixed ambulance crew as it tried to find secure stances to lower the stretcher. Suddenly a rope of three Poles tore loose from the others and began sliding down the wall. De Booy, with lightning-fast reflexes, snatched up the loose end of their rope and belayed it across the longer rope holding Corti's sled. While everyone stopped breathing, the heavy rope gave elastically, and held.

Soon a sort of rhythm was established by a half dozen of the best climbers in the crew, and several hundred yards were covered rapidly. With the rescue party working its way downward, Cassin and Mauri detached themselves for a few minutes and crawled on their hands and knees to the overhang where they had made voice contact with Longhi on the way up. They shouted across the gale, and Longhi, his spirits sustained by the promise of rescue, called weakly back: *"Venite! Venite!"*

"Coraggio, Stefano!" Cassin called. "Try to keep your hopes up! We return for you in the morning!"

As they hastened back to catch up the descending party, Cassin and Mauri heard the parting words of their comrade from Lecco. *"Fame!"* he was calling *"Fame! Freddo!"*

Up on the summit, the Swiss crews gradually found themselves losing control in the gathering storm. By four o'clock, the full brunt of the blizzard could be seen poised just above them and to the north; snow was falling already, and Friedli gave the order to cease the operation. The rescue equipment was hastily stowed in the bivouac holes, and Friedli went on the radio to call the Kleine Scheidegg observation post. Wracked with exhaustion and lack of sleep, and suffering, along with the other members of his crew, from a terrible, debilitating hunger, he told von Almen: "We are going down the west flank to find a bivouac for the storm. If we stay here, more lives will be lost." At 4:30 P.M. he signed the mountain top radio station off the air.

Rain was falling heavily in the valley when this last call had come from Friedli. Already the hundreds of death-watching tourists had abandoned the coin-operated tele-scope on the terrace and had gone into the shelter of the hotel to group around the piano, sip their drinks, and sing. Disconsolate, von Almen and his helpers ordered the radio equipment carried up to the Eigergletscher Hotel, where an attempt would be made to establish contact with the men coming down. Then the balcony telescope was covered over in the rain, and the observation station deserted.

At 5:20 P.M., *Life* magazine correspondents Robert Kroon and Alex Des Fontaines crept out on von Almen's balcony for a final unpromising look through the rain. As though for a last-act encore, a clear avenue opened in the billowing clouds, and they could see all the way up to Longhi's perch. There, standing in the center of the ledge, was the imprisoned man, clearly visible in his fire-engine-red tricot, his face turned upward to the skies, his arms out-stretched as though asking the heavens for a miracle. Then the clouds came together again, and the rains beat harder, and a sudden darkness fell over the valley and the mountain.

By six, the radio equipment had been carried by train to the Eigergletscher. The first news was bad. The retreating rescuers had been able to bring Corti only five hundred yards down the west wall before the full force of the storm had caught them. Now they could go no further.

CHAPTER FIFTEEN

At first, there were sheets of rain; within thirty minutes of leaving the top, every man was drenched through. Then this changed to heavy, soaking snow which stuck wherever it landed. It mantled the parkas and trousers of the descending rescuers, glazed their faces, and blew into their noses and mouths. Soon their eyebrows were whitened and their eyelashes matted with ice. The ropes had absorbed the wetness and hardened, cracking as they were hauled into place. Snap links froze up and had to be hammered open. Now darkness came, relieved only by incendiary flashes of lightning, crashing into the rocks all around them.

Terray and de Booy, tending the sled to which the unconscious Corti was strapped, went ahead to Gramminger. "What do you think?" de Booy asked.

"I am afraid for some of the others," Gramminger shouted above the storm. "There have been close calls already."

"But what can we do? It would be worse on the summit."

"We will have to make a bivouac for the night."

"There is no place to bivouac."

"Then we will have to make a place."

But there were no rocks big enough this high on the west wall to protect all these men against the weather. A short distance farther down, they found one fairly large outcropping. On a level area at its base, they laid the sled bearing Corti and attached ropes and pitons to the rock for security. The wind whipped across the sled, but at least Corti would be protected from the full brunt of the gale by the bivouac sacks tied over him. The faithful Terray volunteered to remain with Corti; the rest lowered themselves farther down the wall looking for other rocks to break the force of the wind. They stopped about 150 feet below, in an area where a few small rocks jutted above the snow, and began covering themselves with bivouac sacks, tent material and sleeping bags out in the open. As Franz Fellerer of the Mountain Guard unwrapped his tent-sack, a burst of wind carried it flapping away into the air. He took up a position on his haunches atop a rock, twisting and turning to keep his face out of the wind, which seemed to come from all directions at once. The others complained and griped and cursed, and a few sang songs at the top of their lungs to keep their spirits up. The wind, becoming colder, stiffened the plastic tent material they tried to put up for shelter and ripped long gashes. Hellepart and Gramminger unlaced their shoes and tried to stitch the cracks, but soon other rips split the crisp material, and finally they gave up altogether, burrowing their heads into their sleeping sacks.

Soon the Swiss group, which had stayed behind on the summit, caught up, occupied with problems of its own. Friedli told Gramminger that they would chance the descent to the Eigergletscher and try to send help up the mountain. Without the hindrance of lowering a sled on the wall, they picked their way skillfully downward in the black night. A short distance above the Eigergletscher station, they met a team of eight Swiss guides, most of them old men who were acting in violation of the anti-rescue policy on the Eiger, but with the noble instincts of Bernese guides of the past. The Friedli group continued past them; the old Swiss guides climbed doggedly upward, but soon were forced to call a halt for the night and make a bivouac of their own in the storm.

Corti, through all this, had remained quiet. But along about midnight, Terray heard loud cries coming from the mound of sacks covering the rescued man. While de Booy hurried up from below to see what the noise was about, Terray clambered around the rock and lifted the covering. Corti's face was contorted with fear, and he was screaming as though in mortal terror. De Booy came alongside. "What is he saying?" Terray asked.

"Sometimes he thinks he is still trapped on the mountain," De Booy answered. "And other times he is shouting that we have abandoned him on top of the summit."

Together they brought the delirious man back to his senses, told him he was safe, and tried to soothe him. Corti's eyes fell shut, and he appeared to drop into a deep sleep. De Booy scurried back down to his bivouac, and Terray climbed around the rock, where there was the tiniest portion of lee from the storm. Hardly had he settled in, squatting on his ankles, holding an outcropping for support, when the screams began again. "Now what is it?" he shouted in French. The noise continued, and once again Terray made the painful visitation to the level area on the other side of the rock, where the anguished Corti could be seen straining upward against his straps. Slowly Terray came to understand that Corti was having sharp abdominal pains and had to relieve himself. "I am sorry!" Terray said angrily. "But this is no time for the niceties of civilization. You will simply have to pretend that you are a baby and use your own devices." He returned to the other side of the rock, but the shouts of Corti went on.

Down below, Cassin and Mauri were huddled together for warmth. They could hear sounds, but they assumed it was merely the whistling and howling of the wind nipping at the rocks. Then, above the storm, they heard Corti shouting: "Riccardo! Bigio!"

"Now what can he want in this awful weather?" Cassin said. The shouts went on. "I suppose I will have to go up and tell him to be quiet," Cassin told his bivouac mate. He found Corti still gripped by the pressures in his abdomen. "Here," the harassed Cassin said, handing Corti a rucksack. "Use this! And please, Claudio, try to shut up!" They were strong words, but Cassin recognized that the entire group was *in extremis,* and the proprieties of drawing-room conversation would have to be put aside.

Now it had been two days since the rescuers had eaten and long hours since they had had anything to drink. The temperature had dropped to twenty degrees; the sticky snow had frozen into a stiff, brittle hardness. "We must have moisture," Gramminger said to his bivouac partner, Hellepart. "Let's try to melt some snow!"

"There is no way to do it, Wiggerl!" Hellepart said.

But Gramminger's needs went beyond reason. He dipped a metal cup into the snow, added some sugar from his rucksack, and tried to soften the mixture by kneading it with his fingers. He ate a little and quickly vomited. "Chocolate!" Gramminger called to Hellepart. "We can eat the snow if we mix it with some chocolate."

Hellepart called, "I gave my last chocolate to the Italian." Ruefully, Gramminger looked at the scraps of bread and salami in his rucksack, still left over from the Friday night drive to Grindelwald, and realized it could not be eaten without moisture. He pulled the tent-sack around his ears and cursed the storm and the Eiger.

Long before sunup, the rescuers threw off their protective coverings and stepped out into the sharp winds and the frigid early-morning air. The storm was whirling away to the southeast, and there were seven inches of new snow on the wall. They gave thanks that the worst was behind them. But was it? They still had to lower Corti five thousand feet to the Eiergletscher station, and then they would have to summon the strength to force back up the west wall to continue the search for the Germans and the rescue drops for Longhi. The poor Italian had now spent nine bivouacs on the north wall, and yet he had been heard just last night, clinging to some small fragment of life, still begging to be saved. He must have survived this final, drenching blizzard. The thought that Longhi was not alive, after all he had suffered, was too painful for the rescuers to contemplate.

Below them, as they broke camp, they heard voices. It was the eight local guides, led by Karl Schlunegger, who himself had made the first Swiss climb of the north wall in 1947, and Hans Brunner, at sixty-two a veteran of thirty years as a guide on the Jungfrau Massif. Exhausted by their own all-night bivouac in the storm, the eight guides drew nearer. Seeing that Corti was well convoyed, four of them turned and walked back down the mountain. Schlunegger, Brunner and the two others joined the rescue group and characteristically asked for assignments. One of them was asked to take Terray's place behind the sled, steering it and belaying it on the ice. Terray, his own amazing endurance now near its end, thanked him and went ahead. By 9 A.M., the party had roped itself down to the "Frühstückplatz," the traditional breakfast stop for parties ascending the west wall. The rescuers were still nearly two thousand feet above the Eigergletscher, with difficult pitches to come, and they were amazed to see a dozen climbers waiting at the Breakfast Bivouac for them. They were Swiss volunteers, skilled amateur Alpinists from nearby towns, and with them was a banquet of food and drink: hot coffee, bouillon, cocoa, soup and sausages. While the rescuers ate ravenously, they saw the familiar figures of Friedli and his Swiss team swinging up toward them from the direction of the Eigergletscher. They must be on their way back up to the summit, to begin new descents for Longhi. But Friedli and his crewmates hauled themselves up to the protective shelter of the huge rock behind the Frühstückplatz, and made no effort to go any farther. For the first time, the members of the descending convoy heard the news:

At 7 A.M., the clouds had cleared, and the telescope crew once again had taken up its watch at von Almen's twin-barreled telescope, now permanently trained on Longhi's perch. But the ledge was curtained in new snow; only a tiny patch of black rock marked the spot. Fifteen feet below, dangling in the ropes left by his companion to protect him, was the still form of Longhi, feet downward, his head resting against a boulder and covered with a thin glaze of ice. The spotters studied the body, looking for the slightest twitch of life. But there was none. A reconnaissance plane went up and confirmed the sad news: Longhi had been swept off the ledge to his death in the terrible storm.

Not long afterward, word came down from search crews high on the northeast ridge of the Eiger. There had been only the slightest wisp of hope that Mayer and Nothdurft had forced an escape across the exit cracks and onto the safety of this ridge on the far side of the face. A dozen parties which had climbed the north wall in the past had reported that great overhangs and rock bulges made such escapes impossible. The only way out, once a rope reached the White Spider, was straight up. But friends of Nothdurft from Bavaria made the search anyway. They found no signs of life on the ridge, and a climbing hut on the route below was empty, the most recent signature in the visitors' book a month old. Now there was no other assumption to be made: Nothdurft and Mayer were dead. They must have fallen down the face and into the litter and crevasses at the bottom, or frozen in bivouac high on the wall.

Friedli ordered cables strung all the way down to the Eigergletscher to give total security to the injured Corti and all the exhausted rescuers. Under normal circumstances, it would have been an easy descent, but he was taking no chances. For all the brave endeavor on the summit, all the lowerings on a cable a mile in the air, all the cold and hunger and thirst, one life had been saved. He meant not to give this life away at the last moment, and he meant also to protect the rescuers who by now were almost walking casualties themselves. It was four o'clock in the afternoon before the painstaking rescue party, assisted by the young Swiss Alpinists who had brought them nourishment, came into sight of the railroad station at the base of the wall. Eigergletscher was a bedlam of sightseers, tourists and journalists who pounced on the rescuers for detailed explanations of what had happened. Friedli was as taciturn as ever, and the rest of the rescue party only wanted to get on a train to go all the way down. "There were a lot of people there who wanted to make business," Hellepart said later, "but we succeeded in avoiding them."

Seeger, Nothdurft's friend from Pfullingen, had been in the descent party led by Friedli, and as he walked out to the station platform he spotted three people standing off to one side, confused by the milling and shouting, and huddled together. He recognized Nothdurft's mother and father and aunt, and walked slowly over to them. "I am sorry," he said. "They are gone." The women wept, and the seventy-five-year-old man nodded his head in grief. Now all his sons were gone. In another corner of the station, Longhi's sister wept alone.

The train came, and the tired rescuers packed their gear and climbed aboard. Terray and de Booy went down to the valley and straight home, their leaves overextended by the rescue. The Mountain Guard napped at the Kleine Scheidegg, then quietly rode down to Grindelwald and drove in the faithful Kombi back to Munich. Friedli and his crew dissolved into the lower valleys, headed for their own towns and villages. The Poles broke their training camp. Seeger escorted the bereaved relatives back to

Bavaria on the train. Fritz von Almen prepared to return to his hobby of searching for chamois on the north face. "If anyone dares focus my telescope on the corpse of Longhi," he said, "I shall remove the telescope and put it in the attic." Max Eiselin made one stop before returning in his new car to Lucerne. He searched out the little red Puch which had taken Nothdurft and Mayer to Grindelwald for their last climb, and removed the note he had attached to the handle bars. "Heartiest congratulations for the Eiger," he read again. "I hope to see you back in Lucerne." He crumpled it up and flung it to the ground.

The black concave saucer of the north wall. Three ice fields are visible (lower half), and the "Spider" shows up as a patch of white near the summit. Note sharp, impassable spur separating north wall from the west wall (right). *Albert Winkler, Bern.*

The Jungfrau Massif; left to right the peaks are the Eiger, Mönch and Jungfrau. *Swissair*

Claudio Corti holds a picture of the tragic Longhi.

Günther Nothdurft. *Walter Seeger.*

Near each piece of mechanical equipment—brakes, rollers. winch—a crew stood guard for security. *Albert Winkler, Bern.*

Two members of the rescue team take a break in an ice igloo on the summit while a third looks for an anchorage for the cable. *Albert Winkler, Bern.*

Perched precariously on the summit ice field, a group of rescuers mans a
radio post. *Albert Winkler, Bern.*

Left, rescuers prepare a pulling path on the ridge while another hacks
away at a brittle cornice of ice, which eventually served as an anchor for
the cable. *Albert Winkler, Bern.*

Franz Fellerer of Munich Mountain Guard crosses summit ridge while work proceeds on lower summit ridge in background. *Ludwig Gramminger.*

Tourists came from miles around to gape at the grisly spectacle through telescopes in the valleys below. *Albert Winkler, Bern.*

Alfred Hellepart, Corti strapped to his back, kicks up the summit ice field toward safety. *Albert Winkler, Bern.*

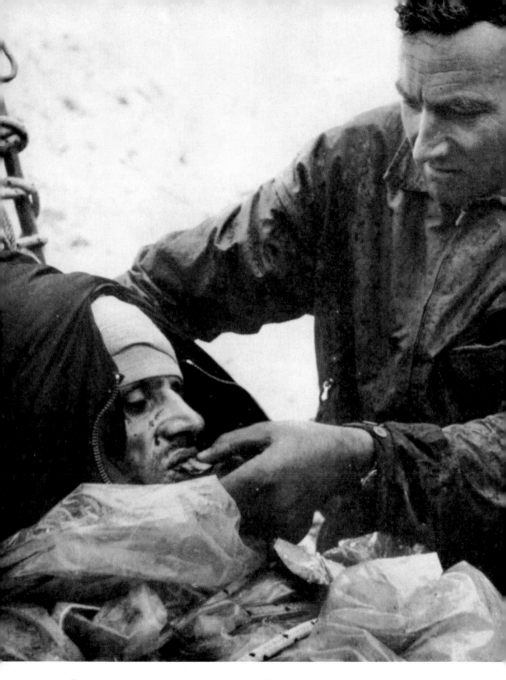

Strapped to a rescue sled on the way down the mountain, Claudio Corti takes a painful bite of chocolate. *Albert Winkler, Bern.*

Lionel Terray, his own strength at an ebb, carries Claudio Corti across the summit of the Eiger as a storm approaches. *Ludwig Gramminger.*

Two members of rescue team haul the rescued Corti down the mountain. *Ludwig Gramminger.*

Cable systems protected Claudio
Corti's final descent to safety.

Yves Debraine

Three of the heroes of the rescue at bottom of mountain next day. Left
to right: Ludwig Gramminger, Lionel Terray, Riccardo Cassin. *Ludwig
Gramminger.*

Lionel Terray.

Carlo Mauri.

Riccardo Cassin.

Robert Seiler.

Christian Rubi.

Yves Debraine   *Yves Debraine*

Left, In the night and day after the harrowing rescue, hero Alfred Helle-part smoked thirty cigarettes, then never smoked again.

Right, Ludwig Gramminger enjoys a chat and a beer the day after the rescue.

A year after the rescue, hero Hellepart was invited to a fête in his honor in Olginate, Italy, Corti's home town. Here Hellepart, center, and Corti, right, walk together in nearby Lecco.

Left, the Corti family—Claudio, Fulvia, and Mariarosa.

Right, Claudio Corti pays his respects to his lost friend, Stefano Longhi.

part two
THE DEAD

CHAPTER SIXTEEN

The body of Stefano Longhi, shackled to the mountain by two ropes, a rucksack flapping eerily a few feet above his head, hung heavy over the people below. There was no way to blot out this scar on the conscience of the Oberland. Fritz von Almen might order his own telescope focused on chamois and ibexes, but no one could keep the thousands of tourists below from lifting their binoculars and telescopes and sopping up the view of the hanging corpse and repeating and embellishing the drearier side of the most spectacular mountain rescue in the history of Alpinism. Soon forgotten in the sordid aftermath was the heroism of Hellepart, Friedli, Terray, Seiler, Gramminger and all the rest. Sipping their drinks in the night clubs and *Bierstuben* of the valleys below, experts and pseudoexperts alike discussed the burning questions: Why had the corps of Grindelwald and Lauterbrunnen guides turned their backs? Why had there been so many errors—the traverse of the Jungfraujoch, the inaccurate positioning of the first cables, the loss of a crucial day, Friday, while "competing" rescue groups rattled around in the valley? Why had Longhi not been saved after so much hope was held out to him? In the comfort of the warm, music-filled rooms below, questions rolled glibly off the tongue. But one question was heard more than any other:

Had Claudio Corti committed an act of violence on the Eiger?

137

Resting in the district hospital in Interlaken, gorging himself on spaghetti and steak, Corti apparently could think only of the mountain which had vanquished him. He showed no overt interest whatever in the fate of his three ropemates. He had lost almost thirty pounds; many of his teeth had been destroyed by the ice he had crunched; his wounds ached dully as they healed. He was soon on his feet, but he walked as though in a trance, his mind still far away and befuddled, his understanding of what had happened on the wall a complete jumble. He gave out wild, rambling interviews, and indeed continued to give them out for months afterward. This simple Italian peasant (of whom Carlo Mauri had once said, "He has a hard time keeping track of his day-by-day activities at home, let alone on a mountain") was a walking case of shocked disorientation.

On Tuesday, the day after special trains had brought Corti from the Eigergletscher station to the hospital at nightfall, a group of three tense men called at the hospital and asked for permission to see the patient. Dr. Walter Bandi told them that only one person could see Corti at a time; the others would have to wait outside. Into the hospital room walked an Italian, Guido Tonella, mountaineer and journalist, who now had taken up residence in Switzerland, where he spent most of his time chronicling the adventures of men and mountains for several European magazines and newspapers. Tonella had come to find out exactly what happened on the mountain. He hoped to be able to answer some of the European newspapers which already were beginning to express their distaste for the bombastic remarks of Corti when he was hauled to safety. (*Der Bund*, a newspaper in Bern, had said, for example: "The 29-year-old Italian, who in the spring of 1956 was extraordinarily lucky in being rescued when he fell off the southwest pillar of the Dru, does not seem to have much respect for the risks and for the courage of the men who put their lives at stake to save him.") A few newspapers had even gone so far as to hint that Corti had been guilty of foul play.

Hardly had Tonella begun his questioning of the punch-drunk Corti when Riccardo Cassin, followed by Carlo Mauri, shoved into the room. Cassin shouted at Corti: "You're the one who should have been left on the mountain, not Longhi!" Corti lay silent on his bed, no trace of expression on his face, and Cassin continued, "If Longhi is up there dead, it's your fault! You wanted him up there!"

"Restrain yourself," Tonella said. "Do not be so rough! Can you not see how weak he is?"

"He is not weak," Cassin shouted back. "He is pretending to be the poor, weak man because he has something to hide. He is trying to avoid paying for what he did! I call him a liar and I call him a faker!"

Corti still made no response, reacting, instead, like a small boy being tongue-lashed by his father. Cassin continued his harangue, and Corti merely pulled the covers up over his neck, mumbling, "Riccardo, please do not be cross with me."

"I will be cross with you!" Cassin stormed. "You are responsible for that poor man hanging dead in his ropes. You, and only you!"

To the surprise of the three visitors, Corti appeared unmoved by this ultimate accusation. In a barely audible voice, he said to Cassin: "Riccardo, what do you think? Do you think they will recognize my success in climbing the north wall?"

This set Cassin off on another tirade. "Did I not tell you?" he said. "Do you not know? You climbed the last three hundred meters *on the back of another man!*"

"Riccardo," Tonella interrupted, "he cannot help what he says. Do you not see the state that he is in?"

Said Cassin: "He is a liar!"

At last Cassin quieted down, controlling the shame and

the anger and the embarrassment he felt over this most sickening scandal ever to come to the climbers of Lecco. It seemed to Cassin that this foolhardy, deadly assault on the north wall had torn down all he had worked for in a lifetime of climbing and had made a mockery of his twelve years of service as president of the Lecco branch of the Club Alpino Italiano. His own career had been a blueprint of the traditions of Alpinism, traditions which taught that one applied the *whole* of one's intelligence and energy to the problem of climbing mountains. One planned with infinite care, seeking the best routes, the most favorable weather, the proper tools and training, and then one struck at the mountain with every resource at one's command. This was the way to climb. One did not cavalierly arrive at the base of an unknown cliff, partnered by an overweight middle-aged man, lacking even the most rudimentary information about the route, and expect to beat one's way to the top by brute force. This sort of vertical Russian roulette was the very antithesis of Alpinism. It was not a question of bravery; all Alpinists were brave, else they would never assay a single climb. Cassin himself was listed in the record books for a long list of first ascents of Alpine faces. But there had never been one attack to which he had brought mere bravery and nothing else. All this he had tried to inculcate into the men of the Ragni, but none of it—not a scintilla—had penetrated the skull of this man lying before him, asking vain questions about how the world would react to his climb, and asking nothing about the fates of the three men he had left behind. "I suppose the best thing that can be said for you," Cassin said, "is that you just do not understand. You make me very sad."

"Our town had a good name in Alpinism," Mauri told Corti in a restrained, almost gentle manner. "Riccardo was the first to give it that name with his good works. But you have soiled our reputation, Claudio. You should have known that Stefano was not capable of going up the north wall." Corti was silent.

Finally Tonella was able to ask some questions. Corti gave ambiguous and vague answers—at this point, he hardly knew himself what had happened on the mountain—and Tonella was able to piece together a fragmentary report for his newspapers. Corti provided the rough details of Longhi's fall, his own fall, Nothdurft's illness, and the departure of the Germans for the top. But he was hopelessly muddled on dates and times, and he showed an almost total ignorance of the correct route to the summit.

Cassin and Mauri drove their Fiat 1100 back to Lecco and found a holocaust of polemics going on. The town was sharply divided. Some of these plain hard-working folk thought of Corti as a great hero, a courageous man who had brought international fame to their community in a brave attempt to climb a wall never before defeated by an Italian. But others said darkly that he was a lunatic, if not a murderer. Even the Alpine club was divided. Long time friends became bitter enemies overnight; there were fist fights and back-fence arguments, and finally the club had to address the matter directly. Cassin and other members asked for censure of Corti. But a majority voted them down. The embittered Cassin, the most illustrious Alpinist the town had ever produced, resigned his post and quit the club.

Similarly, the rescue on the Eiger began to produce a torrent of tangled speculation and accusation in newspapers all over Europe. "The press twisted everything that Claudio said," Alfred Hellepart was to claim years later. But the press was not entirely to blame. The very circumstances of the rescue had made pure accuracy an impossibility. The most skilled linguists in the Swiss press corps found themselves hard put to get an orderly story out of the reluctant, tired rescuers speaking a cacophony of languages and dialects. Friedli, who perhaps had the best over-all picture of what had happened, clung to his pattern of modest taciturnity. Seiler had almost nothing to say, refusing even to give the names of his teammates. Terray and de Booy were back in the privacy of their homes the day after the rescue. Gramminger and the Mountain Guard maintained their traditional position of silence, agreeing to report the details to their own authorities in Bavaria, but refusing to talk to anyone else about what had happened on the mountain. In the face of all this, the press was limited, more or less, to what it had been able to see through the phalanx of clouds and mists scudding around the north wall, and to what Corti could tell them. It soon became obvious that Corti could tell them almost nothing that made sense. He misplaced the time of the first meeting with the Germans; he reported that the Germans lost their food *and* their climbing gear at the first bivouac, only later correcting the statement and claiming that it was the food sack alone which had tumbled down the mountain. He said the Germans climbed out of his sight on Friday; later he said it was on Thursday. He said they left at three in the afternoon; he said it was at nine in the morning. He referred to almost every check point on the mountain in Hinterstoisser nomenclature, glibly referring to the "Hinterstoisser Traverse," "the Hinterstoisser pitch," "the Hinterstoisser chimney," the Hinterstoisser this and the Hinterstoisser that, revealing an almost total lack of knowledge of the face he had sworn to climb. Journalists reviewed Corti's reports, saw the contradictions leaping from the pages, and theorized that he was covering up. It did not matter how loudly he protested his innocence; he himself had admitted that there had been long periods of black-out on the mountain. Who would ever know (including himself) what parts of his story were true and what parts were hallucination? He had imagined, for example, that he had heard someone calling "Corti! Corti!" for the few hours before Hellepart came into sight. But

Hellepart had not called his name; indeed, Hellepart had been under the impression that he was approaching the tent of the two Germans. And if Corti hallucinated things like this, could he not have hallucinated the tale about the Germans' going up the mountain to seek help? Stunned by the blow on his head and disoriented by his long nights in the fantasy world of the mountain, could he not have committed some act of violence, some perpendicular felony, while in a temporarily insane stupor? Thus the argument ran, buttressed by the highly visible errors and impossibilities in Corti's own reports. So it was inevitable that some of the more sensational European publications would conclude that Claudio Corti was not merely a confused victim of a sort of traumatic amnesia, but a liar. And if he was lying, why? The answer was simple: Because he had committed a criminal act on the mountain. Now he was spinning a long skein of falsehoods in an attempt to keep from being found out.

Slowly the journalists began to pick Corti's stories apart, a task which required no vast acumen. And slowly they began to suggest in print that a crime had been committed behind the shroud of the Eiger north wall by the strange, cold man from Olginate whose face showed a continual look of contempt and who did not seem to care at all about the deaths of his ropemates. One of the newspapers presented its own hypothesis, as follows: Corti and Longhi had gone up the mountain with a monomaniacal compulsion to be the first Italians to its top. They had fumbled and frittered around the lower slopes for two days when the skillful German team, only a few hours under way, had caught them. But the Italians would not allow the speedy Germans to pass. This explained the visible slowness of the two ropes crossing the first ice field. Finally the Italians came into difficulty. The Germans pulled alongside, and Corti, in his frustration and rage, still refused to let them by. There was a fight, and the muscular Corti flung the German youths off the mountain to their deaths.

Another newspaper allowed an understandable error of visibility to serve as the basis for an equally lurid theory. On Friday and Saturday, when viewers had observed Longhi on his perch and Corti sitting outside the red tent three hundred feet higher, it was naturally assumed that the two remaining climbers were inside the tent. For two days, the press, limited to its peephole view of the scene, had referred to the "three men at the tent." They had, in fact, merely been seeing Corti and the tent; there were no other humans there. But it had been an easy mistake to make; Corti, changing from his red woolen shirt to his black climbing jacket as one or the other dried out, appeared from the valley below to be more than one person trapped on the ledge. Several days after the rescue, a Swiss newspaper published a photograph alleged to have been taken Saturday afternoon, at a time when Corti later claimed the Germans already were gone. The picture, eventually proved to be totally inconclusive, purported to show three climbers at the tent. From that, an imaginative writer drew the conclusion that Corti, in his half-crazed condition, had heard Hellepart calling in German on the morning of the rescue; assuming that the German-speaking rescuer had come only to save Mayer and Nothdurft, Corti had pushed them off the ledge.

There were other theories no less bizarre. Even some segments of the Italian press now turned on Corti. Cassin was widely quoted as making, in the heat of anger, a statement which disturbed Corti more than any other: "In the mountains, only dead men are left behind." One Italian magazine claimed that Corti had made serious blunders on the face, had been guilty of extreme negligence in accepting Longhi as a last-ditch ropemate, and in general had been the villain of the tragedy. If it had been possible to lower Longhi

fifteen feet to a ledge, the magazine argued, then it should
have been possible to lift him upward to another, safer
ledge. The tone of the articles was clear: that Corti had
abandoned his friend to save himself. Corti threatened suit;
a lawyer from Rome agreed to take the case without fee.
The matter was dropped after the magazine allowed Corti
to tell his side of the story in an article. But even at this late
stage, Corti was contradicting himself. He still had no certain knowledge of what had happened on the mountain.

The most deadly, cold criticism of the climb came from
Germany, where it was immediately assumed that brilliant
mountaineers like Mayer and Nothdurft could not have
gone to their deaths on the Eiger unless there had been some
sort of foul play. Nothdurft's friend, Walter Seeger, spoke
for all of Bavaria when he said: "It is very clear, when you
read Corti's contradictions, that he is hiding something."
Convinced a priori of Corti's guilt, the Germans set about
providing the proof in an orderly manner, allowing others
to theorize. It was known that Nothdurft kept copious daily
notes on the events of each climb, even when he was in uncomfortable bivouac high on a face. Find Nothdurft's body,
they concluded, and the diary would tell what really had
happened. A team of climbers from Stuttgart rushed to
Grindelwald to search for the bodies. But heavy mists clung
to the face, and their time ran out before the Germans could
get any distance up the wall. Later another team of Germans combed the base of the wall but failed to find a single
clue to the fates of their countrymen.

Soon Corti found himself being questioned by policemen,
private and official, in his little row-house in Olginate. He
told them he could add nothing, and referred them to his
lengthy handwritten report to the Club Alpino Italiano,
written, he said, "in the name and service of truth!" Despite
his statements in the report that he had thoroughly studied
the face in advance, his own description of the climb

showed otherwise. It was almost impossible to identify certain well-known pitches on the mountain from his report, and once again dates and times were demonstrably wrong.

The Germans pushed their study. To Grindelwald came Dr. Hermann Lutz, a South Württemberg police official, to make an independent investigation. He called on the police of Bern, and was told that the controversial photograph purporting to show three climbers at the red tent on Saturday actually showed nothing conclusive; one could see anything one wanted in it. Lutz, a member of the Tübingen section of the German Alpine Club, turned then to the matter of the fallen rucksack. He observed that it was inconceivable to him that the two experienced young Germans would have continued an ascent of the north wall without food. "Everyone who knew the two climbers is of the opinion that after seeing their rucksack fall they would definitely have climbed down and never risked an attempt on an exceptionally difficult face without food," he reported. "I myself cannot believe that Nothdurft, whom I knew personally, would ever have risked climbing on without food, after giving serious thought to the matter."

Nor could Lutz understand why the Germans had been willing to give Corti their tent-sack when they had pushed on toward the summit after the accidents. "The giving of the tent-sack to Corti was a comradely mountaineering gesture on the part of the two Germans," he wrote. "All the same, to climb on without food or shelter in the face of an imminent thunderstorm would seem, when quietly considered, an almost suicidal thing to do. It looks as if the two Germans, when they decided to go on, were bent on reaching the summit quite soon or else getting off the face somehow and managing to get help for their teammates reasonably quickly. Yet it seems almost impossible to believe that they could have cherished any such hope after the past days of struggle against the face."

With nothing more to go on—Longhi's body still hung five thousand feet up the face and the bodies of Nothdurft and Mayer could not be found—Dr. Lutz returned to Württemberg with no real case against Corti, other than the Italian's own contradictions and confusions. "Not only the parents, the Tübingen section and all mountaineers interested in the fate of the unfortunate climbers, but I myself would be grateful for any further light on the mystery of their death," he wrote. "Somehow, I think, the ultimate truth will never see the light of day. Those who died will keep to themselves the secret of their last hours." He was wrong.

CHAPTER SEVENTEEN

For every person who accused Corti or hinted darkly that the truth would someday out, there were others who took the position that the truth had already been laid bare, that the inconsistencies and errors in Corti's reports were merely the ramblings of a man who had endured a shattering experience, and that his story was as accurate as one could expect of such a man under the circumstances. Gradually, as Corti's memory returned, some of the discrepancies were cleared up. He had, for example, reported that he had spent sixty-six hours alone in the red tent waiting for help. Under the circumstances, it would not have been surprising if he thought he had been sixty-six days in that cold, plastic tomb. He had, in fact, spent something over forty hours on the ledge. His memory blotted out by concussion and coma, he could only take the word of those who had observed him from below. As far as any matter of foul play was concerned, the number of hours made no difference. He clung steadfastly to his story about Nothdurft's illness and argued that this was the key to the slowness of the climb and the eventual disaster. Nothdurft's mother reported that her son had never suffered from stomach trouble; Corti replied that no climber was immune to the tiny grains of glacier dust which got into the food and water and upset the gastrointestinal system.

Soon the voices of others were heard. One would have expected that those most critical of the truck driver from Olginate would have been the men who had had to climb the mountain and risk their own necks to save him. But the opposite turned out to be true. Lionel Terray was interviewed at his home in Chamonix.

"Listen," he said, "as long as there are so many theories flying around, I will give you my own. It is very difficult to follow what Corti says because he is not a very well-balanced man and he is not a very intelligent man. Sometimes he says one thing, sometimes he says another. But one can accuse him of being unable to tell a straight story without going one unnecessary step further and accusing him of being a criminal. The question is asked over and over. Did Corti do anything to Mayer and Nothdurft? I say he did not. Corti needed the Germans after he had taken the stone. The cut we found on his forehead: that was not a fabrication. He needed every bit of help he could get. Now people say that Corti's ambition was so strong that he might have harmed the Germans to keep them from reaching the top without him. I say this is imagination. In a wall like this such a thing could not be done. Even if men are bad, they cannot feel jealousy toward one another when they are on a wall facing death. Only a madman or a devil could act like that, and I do not think Corti is either. When men are on a wall, they are interdependent. You cannot do evil on a wall even if you are an evil man."

Gramminger's voice, speaking out of three decades of experience in the mountains, came down from Munich: "I knew Nothdurft quite well, and at first I could not understand how he could be on a rope which had moved so slowly. But now I understand. The sickness explains it all. Now it is apparent to me that Mayer and Nothdurft went ahead, as Corti explained, but they lacked the strength to get out of the exit cracks and they were caught in that awful storm. I think that they are up there right now, their bodies frozen to the wall through the winter and held in place by their own ropes and pitons in the summer. Someday they will come down. Everything comes down from that rotten face."

Seiler agreed, and Eiselin came to the same conclusion. "The idea that Corti undertook some sort of a crime is absolutely foolish," Eiselin said. "The psychological situation on such a face makes this impossible. It would not be an advantage to him, but the very opposite. It is true that Corti mixed up a lot of dates and hours. I know other climbers who cannot keep things straight, even on the most routine, uneventful climbs. And one must remember that Corti had been hit with a rock and had had to endure eight bivouacs on the face. Even after a single bivouac up there, one is not in the best of shape physically or mentally."

There remained those who had never suspected Corti of criminality on the wall, but who could not find it in their hearts to forgive him for taking the unqualified Longhi to the Eiger. Not surprisingly, most of these were Italian Alpinists themselves. Cassin, who later mellowed toward Corti, said, "Claudio will always have to bear this guilt. Poor Longhi was nothing as a climber. He had always been in the mountains, but he had not even climbed a single ten-thousand-foot peak. To take a man like that to the Eiger north wall was an act of total irresponsibility."

Mauri, a gentle man who also made eventual peace with Corti, said: "Claudio committed the first and cardinal error: going to the mountain with poor Stefano. He was a good man, Stefano. He labored his eight or ten hours every day; he had no pretensions; he had a sick wife whom he treated with kindness. He did not go to the Eiger with the intention of dying. I suppose he thought that now he was forty-four years old and he had worked so hard and it was a little temptation for him; he might become famous for climbing the Eiger north wall, and he might be loved more by the people of Lecco and every place else where they value climbing feats.

"He must remain on Claudio's conscience. The first time that Stefano spoke of his doubts, Claudio should have headed down the mountain with him. Brave men become unnerved in the mountains, and if they lack skill, their fear will kill them.

"It was Claudio's fault. He is like a little boy. He must do what he must do. The others put too much faith in him; I suppose the Germans thought to themselves, 'Well, here is a strong man from the famous Alpine center of Lecco; surely we will be safest if we stay with him.' And this was their own terrible mistake. If they were the expert climbers that all the Germans say they were, they should have recognized that Claudio was not the man to lead such a rope, and they should have gone back down. It often happens on a mountain that a weaker rope finds a stronger one and uses its strength. But this cannot be done on the Eiger. Each rope must have its own strength and its own faith."

No one questioned the right of all these men to speak; the rescuers had paid for the privilege by long nights of hard, dangerous labor on behalf of their fellow human beings. The bereaved citizens of Württemberg were reckoned more than justified in making their investigation into the deaths of Mayer and Nothdurft, and were even assisted by the Swiss police. The newspapers, including the wilder ones which seemed more interested in sensation than reality, had their traditional right and obligation to examine all the possibilities. And Cassin, as president of the Lecco section of Club Alpino Italiano, was only carrying out his duty to Alpinism and his home community when he cross-questioned Corti sharply. But what was this pronunciamento that suddenly popped up in the Swiss newspapers, beginning with the modest statement that "this is not intended as a biased criticism of the dead men, and if, in spite of that, we venture to state our views, they are intended simply as a warning for young climbers, who may still come, not to risk their promising young lives . . ."? It was the official statement of the corps of Grindelwald guides, the same guides who had steadfastly refused to take any part in the rescue, and who now were stirred to life by a few broad hints in the Swiss press that they had not lived up to the standards of their forebears in the Oberland.

The guides said: "We admit that the climbers involved were above the average in skill. They were picked men from the 'extreme' school of 'specialists'; but their experience was gained on rock, not on ice. And this feature was very noticeable during the climb; for it was established from favorable observation points and by independent observers that the victims when on ice or frozen snow hacked regular bathtubs of steps, and were consequently far too slow on the ice passages. Add to this the fact that the northwall is always being underestimated. The men who first climbed it had studied its problem most thoroughly; they knew its topography by heart, and in spite of that we learn from their reports and those of later successful climbers that they had definitely underrated one pitch or another. This year's aspirants are also reported to have made a searching study of the face. Why, then, did they repeatedly lose their way on it?"

This gratuitous and slightly erroneous analysis of the fatal mistakes of others by a group of guides who, almost to a man, had looked the other way, stirred a hornet's nest of dissension. The *Neue Zürcher Zeitung* jumped into the fray with an accusation that the behavior of the guides had been abominable. Out of his corner to return the fire came a red-faced, elderly man with pale-blue eyes. Christian Rubi, the organizer and leader of the Swiss Guides' Association, was a man who had come up in the world since watching Tony Kurz die in his ropes on the Eiger twenty-two years before. Now a violent debate began in the little valley. It went to the very heart of the guides' attitude, and it rocked the Bernese Oberland to its sturdy foundations.

The Swiss had not had a war since 1847 (and that one had lasted only three days), but this did not mean that they were a totally peaceful people. Their battles were fought with words and votes against one another, and they went on almost continually. In the Lauterbrunnen area, for example, a war had been waged for many years between Fritz von Almen Sr., father of Kaspar and Fritz Jr., and the famous guide, Christian Rubi. As in most such feuds, there was right on each side, although neither would admit it. Von Almen represented the old aristocracy, the landed gentry, the people who sent their sons abroad to school and counted their wealth in the millions of francs. Rubi, who came from the ski-resort mountainside town of Wengen, up the cogwheel tracks from Lauterbrunnen, took unto himself the role of champion of the working classes. It seemed to him that the guides of Switzerland were being exploited by hotel owners and merchants who were raking in a disproportionate share of the tourist dollar. Rubi turned socialist and set about organizing the guides. After many battles, some of them with the archenemy von Almen, he brought six hundred guides into his union, set minimum fees and other protections, and was hailed as the working guide's hero. Later, he was named to the National Council, the Swiss version of the U.S. Congress.

In the ensuing years, it became almost automatic that von Almen would oppose anything Rubi did, and vice versa. As each man grew older, the political skirmishing simmered down, and the lifelong feud became sharply focused on one highly visible, highly inflammatory landmark: the north wall of the Eiger. Their contrasting backgrounds gave the two men different points of view about the face. Von Almen, in his role as the representative of the "finer" things in life, was intrigued by Alpinism of all sorts, including the Iron Age mountaineers who attacked the north wall. He ordered each of his sons to climb to the summit of the Jungfrau,

the Mönch and the Eiger (but not by the north-wall route)
while still barely out of their teens, and he saw to it that
they were trained in what he regarded as the best traditions
of Alpinism.

Rubi, as a "working man" of the mountains, was not
exalted by the Alpine mystique; he represented the old-line
guides, and, to them, the mountains were where they made
their living. He made only slight attempts to understand the
new rescue techniques brought to mountaineering by men
like Gramminger and Friedli. He frowned on acrobatic
climbs involving rope ladders and ice-pitons and other
fancy equipment; indeed, he stood in stark opposition to
any change which would increase the risk to climbers and,
ultimately, to his guides. He was, at once, a liberal in poli-
tics and a conservative in Alpinism.

So it seemed to Rubi, and to the guides in his organization, that the north wall was a sore spot, a place to be
avoided. And the most bitter pill to take was the fact that
every time a rope came into difficulty on the face, tourists
rushed from miles around to that mecca of morbidity,
Kleine Scheidegg, there to fill up the hated von Almen's
hotels and send thousands of francs through the old aristocrat's cash registers. It was easy for Rubi to mistake the
effect for the cause; soon he began to act as though von
Almen was the inspiration for the climbs, and to blame
von Almen when things went wrong on the wall.

CHAPTER EIGHTEEN

It was true, of course, that the von Almens profited from the tragic history of the north wall. Every time a rope became stranded, journalists would arrive in the valley and board the cogwheel train for the Kleine Scheidegg hotels. It was, after all, the best vantage point. There they would file daily running accounts to all parts of Europe, and every story would begin with the dateline: *Kleine Scheidegg*. And Kleine Scheidegg could mean only one thing: the complex of hotels owned by the von Almens. Europeans who did not know the name of the grandest hotels in Paris or Rome knew well the name of the Kleine Scheidegg hotels; they had read it so often in accounts about the north wall.

But it was not true that the von Almen family was happy with the situation or was exploiting the deaths of mountain climbers for publicity space in the newspapers. No one could stop the climbers; most of them, like the Corti rope, acted in complete secrecy; their attempts to climb the wall were *faits accomplis* by the time they showed up in the telescopes below. Under the circumstances, there was little the von Almens could do. They operated a public hotel; they could not set up a screening system, barring the morbid and the sensation-seekers and admitting only bona fide vacationers with skis on their backs. They could not deny rooms to visiting reporters, and they could not rudely turn aside requests for information by the press. What was happening was happening; they refused to pretend that there was nothing on the wall but chamois and ibexes. They benefited from

155

the publicity, but they did not seek the publicity. Indeed, they themselves bore a certain resentment of some of the poorly motivated men who attacked the wall. But the von Almens were only hotelkeepers, not judges.

Rubi's feelings against the von Almens and the north wall soon were felt and reflected by men in his guides' union, and a bad atmosphere was established all over the area. This feeling became a major factor in the 1957 rescue and the failure of the guides to take part in it. "It is your mountain," the guides had seemed to say to von Almen when the Corti rope came into difficulty. "You take care of it."

But the battle lines were etched even more deeply than that. Rubi and his mountain guides' union found themselves not only in direct opposition to the von Almens, but also to the elite amateur Alpinists. It is a peculiarity of unionism that honest labor organizers, acting on impulses of common decency and a desire for fairness and equality, often wind up in their old age as defenders of a new status quo almost as harmful as the one they originally campaigned to correct. So it was with the guides in Rubi's union. They righted all the early wrongs, secured for themselves a living wage and the basic securities, and then clung to this new status quo with every means at their command. They resisted and lampooned every new technique of Alpinism and rescue. The Iron Age mountaineering, involving steep ascents and skilled use of special equipment, caught them up and quickly left them behind. Instead of trying to learn, the guides huddled in their little shells of tradition and pretended that nothing new had happened. There were only a few exceptions. Hermann Steuri, a middle-aged guide of the Grindelwald valley, learned about cable rescues and set up a training course in his climbing school. On the first night of the free course, five of the 140 guides in the area showed up. The next night there were two. On the third night, Steuri was alone. The guides did not want to change. Inheritors of a long tradition of heroic achievements and courageous rescues, they preferred to lead their clients up the well-worn paths of the lower slopes. In the winter, they strapped on skis and called themselves "ski instructors." Others could take over the dangerous rescue attempts on the sheer faces of the Oberland.

With the guides fully committed to this unprecedented policy, the resentment began to go both ways. Elite amateur climbers looked down their noses at them and despised them for their backwardness. Indeed, it was questionable whether the amateurs who made the 1957 rescue would have accepted the aid of the Swiss guides had it been proffered. Rubi claimed for years afterward that some of the guides had volunteered their services to Friedli, and Friedli had merely ignored them. Seiler spoke frankly about it. "There was too much bad blood," he said. "I knew the Bernese guides, and their attitude was so bad compared to the time fifty years ago when the guides were the best men in their villages. When we began the rescue operation, I thought about using these guides and I deliberately avoided them. None came to help, and I was glad. I knew they were not good technicians with the rope and the cable. I was the father of a family and I preferred to trust my life to comrades I knew and not be at the mercy of guides who did not want to learn the business of rescue."

Christian Rubi, in his missionary role as guardian of the guides, could not sit calmly by and accept statements like this. Without an answer, the snowball would keep rolling. Already the Swiss press had expressed shame over the role of the guides, and there were even a few hints in the foreign press that they had not acted in the traditions of their ancestors. Rubi, a skilled writer and experienced debater, struck back. But he did not confine himself merely to a defense of the guides; he launched a bitter attack against the techniques, motivations and abilities of the entire international rescue team. "To be sure," he said, "some of them were brave. But bravery is not enough." He attacked the steel-cable system of rescue. He called the decision to cross the Mönch at night an incredible blunder, one which caused the loss of at least one full day. He charged the amateur rescuers with refusing to call on the guides for assistance. He argued that the six-hour transport of Corti from the Breakfast Place down to the Eibergletscher should have taken, at most, an hour. And he sought to put all the blame on Willi Balmer, the hapless shopkeeper of Grindelwald who had refused to order the guides to the mountain. "All rescue operations are organized by the Swiss Alpine Club sections," Rubi said. "That is absolutely clearly regulated. It was Willi Balmer's responsibility, as chief of the Grindelwald rescue section, to order the guides into action. If a guide is not ordered, he does not go. He should not go. The guides had no orders; they were ready to go and they wanted to go, but they had no orders. If twelve or fifteen of our best guides had been ordered up the west wall on Friday night, they would have rescued Corti Saturday morning, and I have no doubt they would have saved Longhi, too. All the guides had telephones; they waited for the phone calls from Balmer, but none came. It was Balmer's mistake; he did not know his business. And everybody lost his head. All this controversy resulted, and the Kleine Scheidegg hotels, as usual, were happy to make propaganda out of it."

Now it was the turn of the Swiss Alpine Club, the representative of all climbers, to answer Rubi. In a long open letter, addressed directly to "National Councilor Christian Rubi," the club's central committee pointed out that the guides could not take refuge in the claim that their telephones had not buzzed. The letter quoted the laws of the canton of Bern: "In case of accident in the mountains, all mountain guides and porters in the area are obliged to go to search and to rescue those in distress, and to put them-

selves at the disposal of all emergency groups." The law
made no reference to orders and red tape; its mandate was
clear: the guides were obliged to help in any way possible.

"But we understand that the guides are not willing to
make rescues on the north wall and risk their own lives,"
the open letter went on. "We also are against such extreme
wall-climbing. But you say that the mountain guide does not
want to push himself forward, to force his help on others
when he is not asked for counsel or assistance. Mr. Friedli
has done his duty. He immediately got into contact with the
Grindelwald Rescue Station and was told that there were
no guides at his disposal.

"You write that out of total ignorance of conditions, a
dangerous and incorrect route was taken and therefore a
whole day was lost. But you do not point out that twelve
men of the Friedli crew had arrived on the Eigerjoch and
had started a rescue action. You said that a group of twelve
who knew the Eiger could have done more than a gathered
group of seventy. This slanders the self-sacrificing rescuers.
They were not only experts who knew the most modern
rescue techniques, but they were also well-known Alpinists."

The trip from the Breakfast Place to the Eigergletscher
was intentionally careful and methodical, the club noted,
"because Corti was not in good shape. A slow transport
was better for him.

"You leave the grounds of correct criticism entirely when
you say that because of the cable system the whole rescue
took too much time. These are contemptuous sounds. Your
malicious criticism is its own judge. We see clearly that you
are against the modern rescue methods. You would have
had time enough to convince yourself of the practicality of
the steel cable devices when your colleague, Mr. Steuri, gave
a course in rescue instruction in Grindelwald. But you preferred for reasons of prestige to stand aside and later to
insult the brave rescuers. It seems obvious that thanks to

your personal influence there is no other place in Switzerland where it is so difficult to convince the guides of new rescue methods."

Finally came the charge which angered Rubi the most: "You have damaged the reputation of the Swiss Alpine Club abroad, and you intended to."

Back came an enraged answer. "You criticize my criticism," Rubi wrote, "and I criticize your slander against the mountain guides."

He repeated his claim that the guides must be ordered before they can begin a rescue; "this system has been proved good in hundreds of rescues and recoveries of bodies, and it will always be used," he wrote. Otherwise, "sometimes you would have too many people, sometimes not enough."

But in another declaration, Rubi came closer to the heart of the matter with an offhand reference. "The mountain guides did not absent themselves," he wrote. "They were not wanted because this was a special case for propagandistic reasons. The impulse of action came from journalists, photographers, and *hotel managers*." Thus the polemics had come full circle, back to the starting point: the decades-old war between Rubi and von Almen, the laboring men and the wealthy men, the resentful and the resented. A single phrase from Rubi's pen had cleared away all the complex arguments about phone calls and orders and technicalities, and reduced the matter to its simplest terms: a Hatfield-McCoy feud deep in the mountains of Switzerland.

The last to be heard, as always, were the rescuers themselves. Most of them had ignored the battle of words in the valley, preferring to let their own actions speak for themselves. Riccardo Cassin made a gracious statement on behalf of the Italians: "What has been done by volunteers from six different nations was an admirable act, without precedent in the history of Alpinism. Certainly, as in all similar cases, we recognize that if they had acted in another way they might have achieved more satisfactory results. But one only sees this when it is too late. Losing Longhi and the two German Alpinists weighs on our hearts, but we Italians will not criticize what has been done. One of our compatriots who was in danger has been saved. All we can do is thank those who spent their time with such *élan* and vitality, and with so much spirit of sacrifice."

In Chamonix, the outspoken Terray published a more blunt statement of his own:

"The rescue on the Eiger has provoked violent polemics in Switzerland, Germany and Italy," he wrote in the journal of the French Alpine Club. "Certain people who preferred not to join in the action are now troubled by a guilt complex and have allowed themselves to criticize the technical organization and even the principle of the rescue. It is true that no human action is perfect when it is improvised. But whatever one might say, there remains the fact that Alpinists of all nationalities, in a spontaneous spirit of human generosity, in a situation apparently without hope, were not afraid to expose themselves to the risk of the most unpromising rescue proceedings, and one life was saved.

"The rescue on the Eiger is a magnificent example of what can be realized with courage, enthusiasm and will. Of course, it was also a great technical and human success. All the rest is only malicious gossip."

Switzerland seemed to agree. Christian Rubi lost his seat in Parliament and went into a sort of semiretirement in his home village of Wengen. Willi Balmer, an unimportant and unfortunate catspaw who had merely reflected the viewpoint of the guides of Grindelwald when he refused to lay on a rescue attempt, decided not to stand for re-election as rescue chief in Grindelwald, and another man took his place.

But somewhere on the Eiger, two young Germans lay

dead. And high above the beautiful valleys the body of Stefano Longhi hung in conspicuous accusation, freezing to the wall in winter, dangling free in summer. There could be no rest in the valleys, no end to the scandals, until the body was brought down, and the two Germans found.

CHAPTER NINETEEN

There was one possibility that troubled all those who were involved in the 1957 drama, main actors and bit players alike: the possibility that Claudio Corti, the left hand of death, would come storming back to Grindelwald and try to recover the bodies of the three victims himself. The elite rescuers were disturbed at the thought because they were not convinced of Corti's ability to stay out of trouble on the wall, and they did not want to have to scurry to the Eiger to make another grueling rescue. The Oberland guides were perturbed at the prospect because it would have been the final proof of their own irresponsibility; traditionally, dead climbers in the Alps were recovered by Swiss guides, not by imported crews from other nations. But the main tone of European thought was that Corti was now under a cloud of accusation, rightly or wrongly, and that he should stand aside, like a prisoner in the dock, while others searched the wall to see if the dead would tell tales. Even the Club Alpino Italiano took this position. After all, it had been Corti himself who had said, "Find the bodies, and they will prove my innocence."

But who would find them? Only Longhi was visible, and he not for long. Within two weeks of the disaster continual snowfalls high on the face began to cover his body and bind it to the rocks. The guides, frantically seeking to salvage some of their self-respect or, at the very least, to remove the nagging advertisement from the sight of gaping tourists, talked about taking the body down. But their traditional methods would not work. The corpse of Stefano Longhi hung a mile up the ice-glazed face. To recover it, they would almost have to make a successful ascent of the north wall themselves, and under wintering conditions. They could go to the top and lower a man on cables, but this was a technique they had already publicly deprecated; to utilize it now would be an admission that they had been wrong all along. So the corps of Grindelwald and Lauterbrunnen guides, preparing to shed their climbing boots and become "ski instructors" as summer turned to fall, felt balked and frustrated. They watched apprehensively as a dozen skilled members of the Baden-Württemberg Mountain Guard arrived on the scene with the avowed purpose of cutting Longhi down and finding the dead Germans. The bad weather kept the foreigners from making any sort of attempt; they had to content themselves with snooping around the litter and crevasses at the base of the wall, seeking bodies or rucksacks or any sort of evidence which would tell what had happened to their countrymen. But there was nothing remotely resembling a clue.

The guides thought of helicopters, but the military soon dispelled the notion. Helicopters did not function efficiently at high altitude; previous attempts to use them in Alpine rescues had only added to the casualty lists. The furious drafts and currents raging up and down the Eiger would make a helicopter flight a precarious venture, and there had been enough trouble on the north wall already. The military also vetoed another suggestion from the guides: that cannons be positioned in the valley below and used to shoot the ropes away. There was no convenient place to mount a gun within range, and anyway, one did not call up the Swiss artillery to recover the body of a dead climber, no matter how much it weighed on the consciences of the people below.

Now the guides began to hear rumors that Corti definitely was coming back to the mountain to recover the body of his friend. From Italy came the magazine *Il Tempo,* and in it was a long, confused story from Corti about what had happened on the mountain. Cluck-clucking anxiously, the guides passed the magazine about and pointed ominously to the last part of Corti's statement:

> There are only a few people who can understand Alpinists. We are victims of fearful hours. We look into the eyes of death, and perhaps it is our own fault that we force others, those who come to rescue us, to look into the eyes of death too. Nevertheless, we want to go back to the mountains. The feeling is stronger than ourselves. No one thinks when he risks his life that he puts the lives of others in danger. No one thinks this because no one wants to admit that a climb might end tragically. If it were not like this, the mountains would have no one to talk to them. There-fore I will go back again. *I will climb up the Eiger to my friend Stefano.*

There were many Germans, too, who were anxious about Corti's plans. They nurtured the thought that there was evidence on the wall, if only it could be found, that the German rope had behaved admirably and the Italian rope had harassed them, perhaps even acted maliciously. They did not want Claudio Corti, the man in the dock, to be the one who got to the bodies first, there to rip up Nothdurft's diary or to tamper with any incriminating notes Longhi might have left in his rucksack. All through the long winter, they watched and hoped that Corti would stay in Olginate. But they need not have worried. Not even Corti would attempt a winter climb of the Eiger; his own plans called for a trip to the face in the summer of 1958, when conditions improved.

But an Austro-German rope beat him to the attempt. In

the last week of July, 1958, almost a year after the disaster, unusually high temperatures prevailed in the valleys, and Longhi's body once again swayed gently in the winds. The rope of foreigners laid out an attack on the north wall with the triple purpose of climbing the face, cutting Longhi down, and finding their dead comrades. There were three in the party: Herbert Raditschnig, twenty-four, an Austrian army guide who had taken part in the 1957 Austrian expedition to the Cordillera in Peru; Hias Noichl, thirty-six, also an Austrian guide and a former Olympic Games competitor, and Lothar Brandler, a twenty-two-year-old Munich electromechanic who would be making his third assault on the wall. His most recent, in 1956, had ended when another rope of two Germans, pushing ahead, had fallen to their deaths, almost taking Brandler and his ropemate with them.

The three-man team was organized and trained with meticulous attention to every detail; there was far more at stake here than simply the thirteenth successful climb of the north wall. Their equipment was selected with precise care, and even included a tiny radio receiver for constant weather reports. Their advisor was Heinrich Harrer, an Austrian who had been a member of the first rope ever to ascend the face, and who himself had expressed suspicions of Corti, based on his own expertise and the Italian's contradictions and errors after the rescue. While Harrer manned the telescope on Fritz von Almen's balcony, the three star climbers began the assault which they hoped would tie up all the loose ends and settle the controversy one way or the other. Harrer was filming the proceedings through a long-range camera, and if anything sensational turned up, the films would be valuable.

The rope climbed with astonishing speed. By eight o'clock on the first morning, the three men had already dispatched a third of the wall and were making their way across the iceless Hinterstoisser Traverse like ballet dancers. There

was not a cloud in the sky; the temperature in the valley
below was close to a hundred degrees. Climbing conditions
were perfect—for any wall but the Eiger. Hot weather
brought comfort to the climbers, but it also sharply in-·
creased the objective dangers of avalanche and rockfall.

By eleven-thirty in the morning, the three climbers were
in the second ice field; Raditschnig took over the lead from
Brandler, and the rope proceeded smoothly upward. Watching admiringly with Harrer in the valley, Fritz von Almen
said, "They are moving at a phenomenal speed: three hundred feet per hour. They should reach the summit by
tomorrow morning."

At four o'clock, Brandler slipped and fell sixty feet, but
his piton held, and he dug his ice ax into the wall and
climbed back to the others, uninjured. By five o'clock the
rope was only one thousand feet below Longhi's body.
Suddenly there was a hollow rumbling from the White
Spider above. Noichl looked up and shouted, "Watch out!
Falling rocks!" The climbers flattened themselves against
the wall. Noichl hung by one hand from his ice ax, directly
in the path of the rockfall. A heavy stone slammed into his
crash helmet, and as he hung on, giddy from the shock,
another slab of limestone fell on the unprotected hand,
crushing it into a bloody mass. When the avalanche was
over, Brandler and Raditschnig hurried to Noichl's side and
found him losing blood rapidly. They dragged him under
a protective outcropping, put a tourniquet on his arm, and
bound it against his chest. Then they made their way to
Sedlmayer's and Mehringer's Death Bivouac for the night,
about seven hundred feet below the ledge which had imprisoned Longhi. At five the next morning, they began the
tricky retreat, belaying the injured man and making skillful
use of the doubled rope on vertical pitches. Shortly after
noon, they were poised atop the Difficult Crack and had
only to rope down to the Stollenloch, the escape-way into

the railway tunnel. There they were met by Harrer and a small delegation of Swiss guides on a "rescue" mission. Helped through the vertical shaft to safety, the three climbers boarded a train for the valley. Noichl went to the hospital in Interlaken where surgeons amputated two of his fingers. "It was only that stupid accident which prevented us from reaching our goal," he said. "I still hope to go on mountain climbing." But Brandler, repelled for the third time by the Eiger, was merely angry. "I hate that wall," he said.

Now the attempt that was to have settled everything became, instead, a *cause célèbre* of its own. The climbers were castigated for risking their lives to conquer a face that had already been conquered twelve times and to find three men who already had been dead for a year. And the Swiss guides were attacked for their own consistently peculiar behavior. Kaspar von Almen said: "Everybody knew that these three expert climbers could get down without help, but still the guides went up to 'rescue' them. By the time the guides climbed out of the safe gallery window, only Raditschnig had a few more feet to rope down. Nobody needed any 'saving.' The guides did not go up there to perform a rescue; they went up to express their resentment of the foreigners. Later, they submitted a large bill to the three men. They even charged for bandages which they had forgotten to bring along. It was not that they wanted to make money. The bill was only a documentation of what they felt in their hearts. The bill was computed by resentment, not by greed."

A Munich mountaineering magazine, *Der Bergkamerad,* was equally critical of the guides' behavior and referred to "a transparent bill sent because of the rescue of Noichl, Brandler and Raditschnig." The magazine said:

"Noichl paid the cost of eleven mountain guides, but only six had been there. They had looked out of the sure hole of the Jungfraujoch Railway up to the descending rope. The whole cost of the railway from Grindelwald to

Eigergletscher was on the bill, even though the mountain guides had free tickets. Then they added some costs of bandaging, for bandages that had been left at home."

Even the Swiss Alpine Club, a dedicated and respected organization, found itself caught in a new backwash of criticism from other countries. After the rescue of Corti, the club had sent a bill of about $1,600 for costs of the rescue. A large portion of the amount covered the high cost of transporting men and materials up the mountain on the Jungfraujoch Railway, mile for mile one of the most expensive train rides in the world. There had been no attempt to secure any recompense for the volunteer guides, but the Swiss Alpine Club had felt that the out-of-pocket expenses should be paid. In this, there had been no question of vindictiveness. The Swiss had simply been acting like the Swiss, bearing out their world-wide reputation for keeping accurate accounts. Called "a nation of hotelkeepers," they were also a nation of bookkeepers. If a customer underpaid by one centime, he received a bill for the amount. If he overpaid by one centime, he received a refund immediately. It was the Swiss way.*

But the Italians and the Germans did not see the matter in the same light. Postcards and letters poured into Grindelwald and Lauterbrunnen, criticizing the Swiss for demanding money both in the rescue of Corti and the "rescue" of

---

* The Swiss are fond of telling this story on themselves:

A Swiss found himself before God. "What do you wish?" God asked.

"I would like lovely white mountains, lakes and lots of snow," the Swiss answered.

God produced the mountains, the lakes and the snow with a sweep of his hand and said: "But you can't live on this. You may have another wish, and try to make it a more practical one."

"All right. Then I would like to have a cow."

The cow appeared instantly. The Swiss milked it and offered a glass of milk to God.

"You are a fine man, my Swiss," God said. "All the others take what I give them and go away. But you were the only one to think about me. I will grant you a third wish. What would you like?"

"One franc twenty centimes for the milk."

the Raditschnig-Brandler-Noichl rope. *Il Giorno,* an Italian publication, wrote on August 14, 1958: "Here and throughout the world, rescues are not made for money unless the person rescued is able and willing to reward his rescuers. On the Eiger, there were sixty guides at one time: German, Austrian, French, Bavarian, Dutch, Polish, Italian and Swiss. Only the Swiss sent in a bill, which was for 1,500,000 lire. The Ragni of Lecco have clubbed together and paid in 300,000 lire on behalf of their friend, who makes that amount in three years."

So now the Swiss were all being tarred with the same brush—the guides for their failure to assist in the rescue of Corti and for their money-grubbing assistance to the German-Austrian rope later, and the Swiss Alpine Club for sending a bill. The matter had assumed the proportions of a national scandal, damaging Switzerland's reputation abroad, and even threatening the tourist business on which the little country depended. And still the bodies of Longhi and the two Germans stayed on the wall to provide a focus for the diatribes and the attacks. On various levels of government, the problem of recovering the corpses was discussed and debated for long hours. But the solution hung from one apparently unreachable peg: no matter what decisions were made, no matter what sensible conclusions were reached, no matter how much help was offered, some human beings had to go up the north wall, or down the north wall, and risk their lives. And no one seemed willing; at least, no one in Switzerland. But now reports began to trickle in that search parties were being readied in other countries. Swiss delegates to an international ski instructors' conference in Zakopane, Poland, came home to report that a Polish team was undergoing extensive training maneuvers and planned to come to the Eiger in the summer of 1959 to recover Longhi and search for the Germans. An Italian team, eighty-three strong, was making the same preparations. The

German Mountain Guard had made official application to
the Swiss Alpine Club for permission to attempt the recoveries. And Claudio Corti was preparing to carry out his
personal mission of bringing down the body of his friend
and clearing his own name. In the spring of 1959, he had
ridden to Grindelwald on his motorbike to make certain
that Stefano was still on the mountain. Then he turned
around and rode all the way to Rome, where he went to an
American air base and asked if they would provide him with
a helicopter and a pilot to assist in the recovery. When the
Americans turned him down, he called on the offices of
several Italian magazines and newspapers, asking them to
cover the expenses of an organized recovery action in the
summer. But there was still resentment and suspicion of
Corti for his role on the mountain, and the publications told
him he would have to scrape together the necessary money
elsewhere. With several companions from Lecco, Corti
went back to the Eiger on the last Sunday of May, 1959,
climbed the west wall, and made a reconnaissance for a
recovery action later in the summer. All this activity did
not go unnoticed. Corti had said that he would attempt the
recovery in August. Now the Swiss guides decided that they
must get there first.

CHAPTER TWENTY

The key man in the Swiss expedition to recover Longhi's body was Werner Stäger, the chief guide of the Lauterbrunnen Valley, a close friend of Christian Rubi, and one of the guides who had gone to the Stollenloch to assist Raditschnig, Brandler and Noichl the year before. In 1959 he was thirty-six years old, a ruggedly handsome man, tanned and strong, with a sharply broken nose and straight black hair. A successful guide, he worked the mountains in the summer, acted as a ski instructor in the winter, and farmed a small plot in the Lauterbrunnen Valley. Like Rubi, he hated the von Almens and deplored the elite Iron Age mountain climbers. "The whole rescue on the north wall," he had said, "was a play of amateurs versus professionals, and good propaganda for the Kleine Scheidegg hotels." Like his fellow guides, he was obsessed by the sight of Longhi hanging up there, but unlike the other guides, he had a plan for getting the body down. He explained later how it all started:

"In the second week of December, 1958, a German company was shooting a television film at Kleine Scheidegg, and I was working in the film. From a point 450 feet up the hill from the cameras, I had to ski down on Lapland skis—clumsy things with points at both ends, no grooves, and very poor bindings. I was standing there with two other guides, Oskar Gertsch and Fritz Jaun. We were looking at the north wall of the Eiger and I knew what was in their minds. I looked up, too, and started thinking of Longhi

172

and the people looking through the telescopes for twenty centimes per look.

"I made my ski run with only one fall. The others laughed, and we stopped for lunch in a cow shed and made tea. I started talking to Oskar and Fritz, and we agreed we should get Longhi out of range of the telescopes. We shook hands on this and promised that no one would know about it until the very day."

This pastoral description of the origins of the recovery action was in reality a revelation of Stäger's innermost convictions; the significant phrase was "out of range of the telescopes." It was von Almen's public telescope, of course, through which the coins were passing, and Stäger had long since assimilated Christian Rubi's attitude that what was good for the von Almens was bad for the guides. But there was, also, in Stäger's nostalgic description of the talk with Gertsch and Jaun, an omission. The idea for recovering Longhi was not conceived on the ski slopes of Kleine Scheidegg, but several months earlier in a meeting with a Dutch journalist, Jaap Giltay. The Dutchman, representing a press service in Amsterdam, had come to the Oberland on a vacation trip, viewed Longhi's body, and learned about the mystery and controversy connected with it. He conferred with Stäger and Gertsch, the chief guide of the mountainside village of Wengen, and was told that money was the main problem. The Swiss guides wanted to recover the body, but they were poor men, and they could not afford the necessary equipment. The two guides said the recovery action would be too dangerous without a large crew of experienced guides, airplanes to carry the guides as high as possible up the mountain, and cable-and-winch equipment for lowering a man down the face. Giltay told them he had an idea how the money could be raised and promised to write to them from Amsterdam.

His plan was to bring several European publications in

on the operation and allow them to do exclusive words-and-pictures stories of the recovery action in return for the necessary financing. There was nothing whatever reprehensible about the plan; it was, in fact, a stroke of journalistic prowess on Giltay's part. Soon he had contracts, and he informed Stäger and Gertsch in March, 1959, that the money would be available. There ensued a long series of letters between the guides and the Dutch editor. The worst that could happen to Giltay would be for other editors to learn of the operation, send their own reporters and photographers to the scene, and effect an honest "theft" of the exclusive story. To guard against this, Giltay included a provision in the guides' contract that called for a fine of $250 for any guide who provided information to outside journalists within three months of the operation. Gertsch balked at this as too stiff. "Why don't we make it fifty or sixty dollars?" he wrote Giltay. He also pointed out that the costs would be high. "Transport of the material by Geiger (airplanes) is very expensive, and we need anchoring material and steel cables, walkie-talkies, airplanes, ten guides, and, as the Alpine Club does not have the material which is necessary for this action, we must count on big expenses," Gertsch wrote. "Therefore we are dependent on the fact that as much money as possible is raised for this." Finally he asked the Dutchman to guarantee the guides a minimum payment "so we are protected." Giltay sent back a revised contract, and, on May 21, 1959, Gertsch replied that the contract would be signed by all the guides taking part. Eighty per cent of the money raised would cover the expenses and salaries of the Swiss guides; the rest would go to the Dutch news agency.

With the financial arrangements proceeding smoothly, Stäger made a reconnaissance flight across the north wall with the ubiquitous Hermann Geiger at the controls. Like an engineer preparing to solve a thorny problem, he took photographs and laid out diagrams showing exactly where the body was hanging and marking the best routes of access from above. Immediately he could see that the recovery party would have one small advantage. The body was positioned so far to the east that some of the work on top could be carried out on the easier northest ridge instead of on the sharp and dangerous edge of the summit. Counting each centime, he calculated that the cable would have to reach 1,300 feet downward; he purchased 1,350 feet, allowing only the smallest safety factor. All these preparations were carried out in the utmost secrecy, following the terms of the contract. But there were, inevitably, a few leaks. The editor of *Der Bergkamerad,* the Munich mountaineering publication, sent an inquiry to Christian Rubi, saying that he had heard reports that the Swiss were planning to recover the body and had already made reconnaissance flights across the face. Rubi, protecting his guides, replied, "As far as I know, Mr. Geiger has invited two mountain guides and ski teachers on a flight because they intend to build an airport up on the Männlichen for small airplanes for the benefit of high Alpine skiers." The Germans were thrown off the track. But soon rumors reached Corti in Olginate that certain European publications were putting up the money for a search of the face. He dashed to the offices of several magazines and offered to place himself at the disposal of the search parties. But the magazines told him that they had no such plans, and even if they did, he would be the last person they would invite to take part. "They told me that I was a criminal," Corti said. "They told me they did not want me near the body of Longhi because they were convinced that he would have some words on him telling how he had been deserted by me. They told me again that I had abandoned Stefano to save myself, and they did not want anything to do with me. I was extremely sad about all this, and I felt helpless. Only the finding of the bodies could clear my name, and they were denying me the right to help find the bodies. So I told them that I was going to the Eiger myself, when the weather was better, and recover Stefano's body with some of my friends from Lecco."

The news of Corti's intentions, and his visit to Grindelwald and reconnaissance of the west wall, crystallized the guides' plans. They selected the first week in June as the date of their own expedition, partly to beat Corti and all the others who were laying plans, and partly because there were certain advantages in such an early attack. It would be cold, and conditions high on the face would be almost wintry. But this would mean less danger from avalanche and rockfall.

In contrast to the hurried improvisation of the rescue of Corti, the guides' operation proceeded cautiously, step by step. On June 6, with several days of clear skies predicted, Stäger called together the twenty-three guides who had signed the contract and ordered them to take the last train up to the Jungfraujoch the next day. Geiger had found two plots of high, level snow for his ski-equipped Pipers. One was near the Jungfraujoch, where he could pick up the expedition members, and the other was within a short two- or three-hour hike of the Eiger summit. Thus the guides would be spared the grueling west wall ascent or the traverse across the Mönch which had so hampered the earlier parties. Utilizing the Geiger mountain-to-mountain shuttle service, Stäger and a few others spent all day Sunday, June 7, ferrying cable and winch equipment to the landing area near the top of the Eiger. They covered the gear with tents, topped the cache off with a Swiss flag, and returned to the Jungfraujoch to give the guides their instructions for the next day. At 3 A.M. on June 8, the expedition members were awakened. The weather appeared to be good, and Stäger phoned to Geiger that all was in readiness. Geiger and his pilots headed the planes toward the landing spot near the Jungfraujoch to begin ferrying the guides. But the peculiar meteorology of the Eiger quickly cut off the operation. Clouds billowed out of nowhere; the guides returned to the safety of the Jungfraujoch and Geiger flew his planes back to the valley. Several days went by; the sky remained dark, and thunderstorms broke incessantly across the face. Stäger told his comrades that he was not optimistic. "We must be absolutely sure of the weather," he said. "We will not undertake any recovery action unless there is at least a three-day period of clear skies and no storm activity whatever. Otherwise it would be crazy."

As the weeks of inactivity went by, Stäger began to see visions of financial disaster. The whole operation depended on secrecy; otherwise, outside publications would get in on the "exclusive" and the contract with Giltay would be voided. The recovery action would cost at least nine thousand francs (about two thousand dollars), and if the contract was breached, the guides would have to bear the expenses themselves. Stäger and Geiger had taken out special licenses to enable them to fly across the face and utilize their short-wave radios; the licenses gave them the exclusive rights to the airspace in front of the north wall, but only for a short term. Soon the term would run out, and the airspace would be available to anyone. Stäger was forced to wait in the valley and hope that the abortive attempt of early June, involving twenty-three men and several flights, had gone unnoticed by his competitors in the international body-recovering business.

A month went by. On July 6, the weather cleared again, and on the morning of the seventh, Stäger called the guides and told them to assemble once again at the Jungfraujoch. At 5 A.M. the next morning, under clear skies, Geiger and his pilots carried the guides across to the landing area on the Eiger, where they shouldered the equipment left a

month earlier and carried it to the summit. The weather
held, and the men picked their way across the summit
ridge to the anchorage position selected by Stäger near the
top of the northeast ridge. By 4 P.M., they had prepared the
anchorage and secured the winch. With their usual caution,
they flew back for one last night's sleep at the Jungfraujoch
Hotel before the actual recovery attempt next day.

At 2 A.M., July 9, with total secrecy still the watchword,
Oskar Gertsch climbed out of bed and shouted, "Time to
get up, boys!" At 2:45, the guides sat at the breakfast
table for a final briefing. Despite their resourcefulness, the
twenty-three-man team had one serious defect: a lack of
knowledge and experience in the cable technique. Stäger
had boned up on the system on a crash basis and had made
a few safe practice drops on the quarter-inch cable. But
most of the men had never used steel devices in rescue work.
A single exception was Fritz Jaun, a forty-two-year-old
bricklayer and guide with a powerful physique and the
calmness and stolidity of the typical Bernese Oberlander.
Jaun, encouraged by Kaspar von Almen, had been one of
the few guides in the area to work out on the steel-cable
devices set up in Hermann Steuri's climbing school. He had,
at least, a nodding acquaintance with the equipment, and
Stäger quickly named him as the man who would make the
descent to the body. Two guides, Alfred Fuchs and Ferdinand Gertsch, would climb down the ridge and position a
set of rollers for the cable; Oskar Gertsch and Jaun would
work their way below this point and anchor a second set
of rollers on the fall line leading to Longhi's body. Then
Jaun would be on his own for the rest of the descent. With
all plans spelled out carefully, the expedition members
hiked to the landing area, climbed into Geiger's three planes,
and began the 9½-minute flights to the Eiger. At 7 A.M.
all were assembled on the northeast ridge, and Stäger

radioed to the observation point at Kleine Scheidegg that the operation would begin in half an hour.

Soon the four men were moving down the ridge. They were protected by steel helmets and in constant radio communication with Stäger, who had taken his high-powered binoculars to a vantage point on an outcropping of the west ridge, far across the face. As a final safety measure, Jaun was equipped with a parachute.

Fuchs and Ferdinand Gertsch positioned the first set of rollers on the ridge without trouble and remained there to clear it if it fouled and secure it if it worked loose. Oskar Gertsch and Jaun, belayed by the cable and ropes from above, made the tedious descent to the point where the final rollers would be placed. En route, they lost their way on the rock-scarred face and had to reclimb a short pitch to find a new passage. They were so laden with equipment, and the climbing was so difficult, that the retracing of their steps cost them an hour of effort. At last, all was ready, and the voice of Stäger came into the headsets: "Now Fritz will have to go down alone. The others must wait at the rollers."

As Jaun began the descent, dangling from the quarter-inch cable, Gertsch called down, "Is everything all right, Fritz?"

Back came the imperturbable voice of the guide: "It seems to me that everything is all right. *Auf Wiedersehen!*" From now on, radio communication would be between Jaun and Stäger, watching from his observation post on the west ridge.

For the first sixty feet all went smoothly and easily. Then Jaun came to sheer vertical walls dropping ninety to a hundred feet without a foothold. There were tiny ledges where he could stop to catch his breath and then straight drops to the next foothold. At 10 A.M., after nearly two and a half hours on the wall, he reached the last cliff above the snow-covered ledge on which Longhi had held out for three days. "Fritz!" Stäger radioed. "Attention! You are exactly over the ropes of Longhi. Keep going straight down!" As the winch crew slowly paid out line, puffs of cloud enveloped Jaun, and Stäger called to the valley for an immediate weather report. The Scheidegg crew answered that light rain showers were predicted for the afternoon. Jaun, hearing the report simultaneously, radioed to Stäger: "Continue lowering away!"

The clouds flitted off as rapidly as they had appeared, and once again Stäger had a clear view of his comrade. "Look down, Fritz!" he radioed. "Now you can see the ropes of Longhi. They are about one hundred feet further down the slope."

Jaun replied: "I can see the ropes. I will arrive six feet to the left of them."

A few minutes later Jaun announced: "Stop! I am there. I can see the ropes at my feet." He reported that the ropes were securely anchored to the wall by pitons, and went down at a slight angle to the ledge before dropping fifteen feet vertically to the hanging body.

Stäger said: "Don't break them! Be careful! Don't break them at the last moment!"

Jaun tested one of the ropes and reported that it seemed to be in good condition. Using a rope as a guide line, he descended to the perch which had imprisoned Longhi. He let himself over the side, and at 10:45 he radioed: "I am with Longhi. He is intact."

Stäger had hoped that the body would have dried out and become lightened from the constant freezing and refreezing in the high winds, but Jaun reported that the Italian seemed not to have lost an ounce of weight. The plan was to put Longhi in a large sack and pull body and guide up together. But Jaun, hanging in space alongside the corpse, could not maneuver all the weight. "He is too heavy," he radioed. "I can't get him into the sack. I will have to bring the body up as it is." He secured lines from the cable to the body, snipped the old ropes which had held Longhi for twenty-three months, and ordered the winch crew to haul away. Six feet up, he came to the rucksack of Longhi, also tied to the old ropes. "Fritz!" Stäger radioed excitedly. "Look inside it! Maybe there is something there to clear up the mystery!"

Jaun's voice began to intone the contents of the rucksack. "An ice ax . . . shirt . . . two hammers . . . crampons . . . a few snap links . . . some dried-up medicines . . . a few scraps of old Italian newspapers . . ." There was silence.

"Nothing else?" Stäger asked.

"Nothing else," Jaun replied. "I am certain."

CHAPTER TWENTY-ONE

Stäger ordered Jaun to leave the ice ax, the hammers and the sack on the ledge. "Now," he said, "we will pull you up." With nearly four hundred pounds on the cable, the ascent went slowly. First went Jaun; about a yard below his feet came the corpse of Longhi, arms flapping loosely, the trunk twisting on the rope which attached it to the cable. The cable, through all the maneuverings, had become tightly twisted, and soon Jaun felt himself begining to spin in his harness; he had to close his eyes to keep from blacking out. Other problems developed. Longhi's body, dragging along behind, was continually wedging into cracks. "Stop!" Jaun called repeatedly. "I have to go back and free the body!" At 11:45, Jaun radioed that he was exhausted, and the first note of doubt crept into his voice. "I don't think I can make it to the top," he called. The winch crew stopped cranking, and for a long time there was no sound from the guide below. Then the voice came through loudly. "Pull me up!" Juan said. "Do you want me to stay down here until tomorrow?"

The cable slowly whirred upward, and soon Jaun could see the white plastic helmet of Alfred Fuchs at the last rollers two hundred feet above. Still to be crossed was a bulge of rock, jutting fifteen feet out from the face. A traverse to one side or the other would have been too danger-ous on the twisted cable; Jaun ordered the winch crew to pull him and Longhi straight up through space to the bulge. Now hanging free in the air, Jaun felt the vibrations as the cable bit into the rock. Spinning and twisting, he fought to keep his equilibrium, and then he realized that he was no longer moving upward. The cable was stuck. "Do something!" he radioed, a note of fear in his voice. The cable began to move a few inches at a time; he grabbed the edge of the outcropping and hauled himself up. The ascent continued but with increasing slowness. The quarter-inch cable had been spliced in 150-foot lengths, and each splice was nearly an inch thick. The cable was cutting deep, narrow grooves, and the thick splices were entering them and jamming. With Fuchs only 150 feet above, waiting to help, Jaun came to a full stop in mid-air, and began a rapid whirl as the stalled cable unraveled its kinks. For long seconds, the world spun around Jaun's eyes. He grabbed for the rock, steadied himself, and tried to pull up. But the load dangling below him held him back. Again and again he grabbed the rock with one hand, trying to diminish the tension on the cable, and with the other hand attempted to free the wire from its tight groove. The winch crew tried to pull the cable up by brute strength, but Jaun, hearing the whining sound as the wire tightened, radioed quickly: "It doesn't help to force it! You only make it worse!"

For an hour and a half, the exhausted guide hung free with his heavy load, yanking and tugging, clawing at the rock, until at last he had lost almost all of his strength. "Stop now, Fritz!" Stäger radioed. "We will have to send a man down to help you."

Alfred Fuchs, tending the last set of rollers, was rigged to a rope and sent down the sheer wall. Reaching the jam after a skillful descent, he drove pitons into the rock and secured another rope to them. Then he lowered the new rope to Jaun, and told him to pull up on it, to reduce the weight on the cable. With the tension slightly lessened, Fuchs grabbed the cable, braced himself against the mountain, and pulled outward with all his strength. The cable whipped free, and Jaun was out of danger again. Fuchs, his hands cut and bruised, remained with Jaun and the body for the climb to the lower edge of the ridge. They arrived at the bottom set of rollers at two-thirty in the afternoon, and Jaun took a short rest. It was an hour and a half later before they had conquered the final three hundred feet up the ridge to the anchorage, and at last, after nearly nine hours in harness, Jaun dragged the body of Stefano Longhi onto the summit. A strangely morose crew of guides met him. They had recovered the body successfully, but it had turned out to be merely a body, not the final solution to the mystery of 1957. And the entire basis for the financial support of the operation was threatened; planes had been crossing the face and taking pictures all afternoon. They were not only Geiger's red Pipers, but other planes hired by competing publications, both magazines and newspapers. The air embargo had run out. Equally annoying, "opposition" reporters had been seen watching the entire operation from the Kleine Scheidegg hotels, and some outsiders had even tuned in on the radio communications. The "exclusive" operation, which was supposed to bring in 9,000 francs to pay the guides, had been open to the public.

Now convinced that all their work was for nothing, the guides went about the distasteful task of dragging Longhi's body 750 feet along the summit ridge and then through the snow to the landing area. It was six o'clock before the body finally was brought alongside the short, snow-covered runway. Stäger made a last search of the dead man's clothes, but all he could find were a lucky charm and the badge of the Ragni. The face was dark brown from the weather; the lips were pressed tightly together; the eyes stared blankly ahead. Stäger and another guide straightened out the legs and arms; as they did, Stäger glanced at Longhi's wrist and noticed a watch. It was running; all the motion had reactivated the self-winding mechanism.

One by one, the unhappy guides climbed into the planes

for the trip to the Jungfraujoch and the descent by train to the valley below. The last flight arrived at eight o'clock; the passenger was Longhi. His body, shrouded in a brown cloth sack, was placed on a flatcar for the trip to Lauterbrunnen. His feet, encased in red socks and climbing boots, stuck out of the sack; piled around him on the flatcar were pitons, ropes, snap links, crampons—the gear of the climbers who had made the recovery. With the clack of the cogwheels for a dirge, the train ground slowly through the black tunnel to its first stop on the downward leg: Eigergletscher. The station was dark, shut down for the night, but suddenly the flatcar was surrounded by fifteen or twenty men materializing out of the shadows. They were Italians who had come to Switzerland to work in the tunnel. One of them threw rhododendrons on the body. Twenty minutes later the train eased into Kleine Scheidegg, and more Italian railroad workers crowded around to pay their last respects to the man whose body had hung over them for twenty-three months. Wreaths were laid gently on the flatcar, and the Italians asked the guides where their countryman would be taken. The guides chomped on their cigars and did not answer. After another hour down the mountain, the body reached Lauterbrunnen. The guides carried it into the *Totenhalle* of the cemetery, where Eiger victims had been taken for twenty-two years. In the little mortuary, Longhi's sister Gina broke into sobs. Over and over she asked Stäger if he had not found a clue, any shred of evidence, to establish what had happened. Stäger took the grief-stricken woman aside and handed her the rope which had held her brother to the mountain. "It is all I can give you," he told her. "I do not know what really happened up there. Let it stand as it is. It makes no sense to question any more."

The next day, Longhi's sister took the body home to Lecco in an ambulance. Doctors examined it and found that one leg was bloated, broken in two places near the knee.

Reporters speculated that the leg had been broken on Longhi's first fall down the mountain. But Longhi had been seen standing on the ledge, moving about, with no apparent injuries to his legs. And Corti insisted that Longhi had made no mention of a leg injury when he was left behind on the perch. Another theory was advanced: that the leg had broken against the wall long after Longhi had died, perhaps in one of the high windstorms that hit the mountain. But this did not explain the bloating. Limbs would not swell if they were broken after death. Only one possibility remained. On his last night on the mountain, after he shouted his final *"Venite!"* to Cassin and Mauri in the advancing thunderstorm, Stefano Longhi must have been blown from his perch, his leg shattering on the wall when he was jerked up against the rope. There, hanging in agony through the night, he had died.

The horrifying knowledge of how Longhi had died renewed speculation in the Italian press about Corti's role. One magazine, *L'Europeo* of Milan, braced Corti directly on some of the more critical points, and the result was an article entitled: *Non Sono Un Criminale* ("I Am Not a Criminal"). *L'Europeo* wrote:

> . . . Nobody knew what happened when Longhi was abandoned and when the Germans abandoned Corti. . . . Corti never has revealed everything. . . . He only has defended himself strongly in the polemics that began soon after the cruel story became known.

The magazine quoted a Swiss guide as saying, "We didn't understand why Longhi was not saved together with his companions"; there were better places to put him only a short distance higher on the face. Corti answered that there was not enough strength left in the party to pull Longhi any distance at all and that the rope was scraping and fraying across the jagged edges of ice. They had tried for three hours to hoist Longhi up, but they had only succeeded in sapping their own strength and risking the life of Longhi with every pull.

But why had he made two major mistakes in climbing the wall? asked the interviewer. "We missed the proper route," Corti said, "because we were influenced and cheated by an old shoe, a crampon and pieces of pitons that we found often, stuff that came from other people who also missed the proper attack route." What about the failure to make the standard "Traverse of the Gods" leading to the White Spider? Why had they climbed above it and selected a far more dangerous traverse? "It wasn't a mistake," Corti answered. "We took a route away from the normal route, going left of the Spider to avoid continuous avalanches."

Why had the rope climbed so slowly? Again, Corti told about Nothdurft's stomach illness. Then he addressed himself to the charge that it was not mere coincidence that he had lost five ropemates in his climbing career. "To those who have said that this was not the first time that I have abandoned a ropemate," he said, "tell them that Corti cannot help it if lightning arrives and passes through the body of his companion. . . . Tell them that I am not a criminal. When Zucchi and I slid five hundred yards down the Petit Dru, I took him on my back like St. Bartolomeo and I brought him out of the ice zone in two or three hours. . . ."

These self-serving declarations from the man who had been spinning conflicting stories about the tragedy on the Eiger did nothing to dispel the notion in certain people's minds that he was a liar or a lunatic. To them, he was no St. Bartolomeo at all but the devil incarnate. They told themselves that someday the bodies of the Germans would be found, and the truth would be known, and this sullen man from Olginate would be brought to account.

"There were twenty-three guides, and all had done their work with no sensation, no publicity," Stäger wrote after the recovery of Longhi. "It was the greatest achievement in Alpine rescue ever made, not only a technical achievement but also an achievement of friendship. . . ."

With similar pompous and inaccurate statements, the Oberland guides continued their almost perfect record of putting their climbing boots in their mouths and converting enterprises of bravery and skill into frenzies of controversy and dissension. The guides had acquitted themselves with courage, but they were not content to let matters rest there. By braggadocio and loud argument, they set themselves up as the equals, if not the superiors, of the amateurs who had rescued Corti, all the while claiming that they had been acting merely in the interests of international friendship and without publicity. The fact was that far less noble motivations had sent the twenty-three guides up the mountain. They deplored the sight of the body on the wall as a symbol of their own shabby behavior in 1957. They resented the continuing publicity harvest reaped by the Kleine Scheidegg hotels. Many of them went along on the trip merely to make money; this was all that had kept them so discreetly silent beforehand. The supersecrecy which cloaked the operation on behalf of the underwriting publications had, indeed, almost brought it to a disastrous end. Because of the secrecy, Stäger and his comrades had not been able to call on Gramminger or Friedli or other experts in the use of steel-cable devices. Thus they were denied valuable advice on the finer points of the technique, and it was lack of knowledge of these subtleties that caused Jaun much of his trouble. All the twisting and spinning in mid-air, for example, would have been avoided had the cable been equipped with Gramminger's swiveling devices which prevented kinking. And the work with the winch would have gone far more smoothly had a few experienced cable technicians been brought in to operate it. Fritz Jaun's nine hours on the wall were a testimonial to his own strength and courage, but they were also evidence of the whole expedition's lack of knowledge of the equipment.

Said Robert Seiler: "When I thought back on what the Swiss guides had said about our own rescue of Corti, after we had had to act with great haste and in extremely poor weather, I could only be annoyed at their recovery of Longhi. They made such a colossal production out of the whole thing, and merely to recover a mummy. They hired airplanes to carry them as far up as possible, when it would have been easy to take the west wall route to the top. They bought all new equipment, some of it of the wrong type, because they knew that expenses were being paid by the publications. They said they had to buy the equipment because it was not available anyplace else. It was available at many places, including the rescue center at Thun, a short distance away."

The Swiss newspapers expressed resentment of the manner in which the expedition had been financed, leading Rubi to declaim: "It was the Swiss newspapers' own fault. Nobody in Switzerland came forth and said they would pay the money to recover the body; 'Here is the money,' or 'Here, we will at least pay for the material.' But when the foreign news agencies came along, the Swiss papers complained."

In Germany, the whole basis of the operation was attacked. *Der Bergkamerad* wrote:

> . . . A dark problem has come up, the fact that we mountain climbers are only sure to be rescued and recovered if there is somebody who pays the costs. It does not matter if the climb is on the Eiger north

wall; it is the same all over the Oberland, where there is no organized rescue crew except the mountain guides who are dependent on money to live on. Longhi would still be up there if nobody had paid. This is a dark point. . . .

When the original rescue was on [in 1957], the Swiss guides behaved disappointingly. They said, "You cannot ask a father to climb the murderous north wall to save other lives." But in 1959 the mountain guides changed their attitude. Fritz Jaun is the father of three small children. His two comrades who helped him up also had little children at home. Why? Because of money.

It seems to us that the mountain guides have now recognized their carelessness and want to improve themselves. But this is only a technical improvement because we still do not know if they will rescue us. . . . It is time for Switzerland to find a way to finance such rescue undertakings by official rescue foundations, to the good and to the profit of the reputation of the Swiss mountain guides. Why is Switzerland, compared to the other Alpine countries, so backward in this?

So the pattern continued. Switzerland had reaped nothing but opprobium from the beginning of the ill-fated climb, and even with the recovery of Longhi, the diatribes continued. Hardly anyone in the other countries remembered—or wanted to remember—that the impetus for the Corti rescue had come from the Swiss, that most of the rescue party had been Swiss, and that the Swiss had a long heroic record of policing their own mountains. All that was talked about now was the bitterness of the guides, their attacks on the rescuers, and their decision to recover Longhi for cash on the barrelhead.

The memory lingered on, mainly because Werner Stäger kept the issue alive by public lamentations that the guides were left holding the bag for the expenses. With the exclusivity of the operation lost, Giltay had found himself hard-pressed to sell the story at the expected high rates and thus pay off the guides. Technically, the contract had been broken, but the Dutchman honored it anyway. The money came in slowly, and payments were made to Stäger's crew. Eventually, Giltay paid out 10,300 francs, more than the amount originally estimated for the expenses. But Stäger complained that costs had turned out to be higher; 3,657 more francs would be needed. When the money was not forthcoming, he set off on a lecture tour of Switzerland, telling all who would listen that the poor Oberland guides were stuck for the balance, about 166 francs per man, and bemoaning the fact that no one in Switzerland would pay. He held two press conferences in Bern, loudly outlining the plight of the guides, and the newspapers carried this final accusation against the entire country. The whining noises reached high levels of Swiss government and business; in those worried circles, it did not seem that the scandal on the Eiger would ever end. But at least they could quiet the guides. On November 3, 1959, four months after the body was recovered, a representative of the Swiss banks wrote to Stäger saying that he had heard that there was a deficit and the guides had had to pay the money out of their own pockets. A week later, Stäger answered the banker, confirmed the report, and noted that the shortage was 3,657.75 francs. The Swiss Foundation for Alpine Research also made an inquiry. Stäger replied on December 4, a month after he had heard from the banker: "Until today, no official institution has asked for the expenses we had. The guides who took part have not been paid for their work, and each one has had to pay 166.25 francs for the remaining deficit." He sent the Swiss Foundation an expense sheet showing the same deficit he already had reported to the banker.

Now matters moved smoothly. Ten days after Stäger's accounting to the Swiss Foundation, he received a letter saying that the organization would pay the full amount of the deficit. Within a month, a check for 3,657.75 francs came to Stäger from a group of four Swiss banks, and a check for exactly the same amount came from the Swiss Foundation. Now the guides were happy. The deficit had not only been paid, but paid twice. With the first check, Stäger reimbursed the guides for the equipment which they had left behind on top of the Eiger. This included a payment of 468 francs to himself and 725 francs to Christian Rubi for hemp ropes. The second check, from the Swiss Foundation, was split among the guides, with Stäger allotting 385 francs to himself. "The greatest achievement in Alpine rescue," the international "achievement of friendship," at last could show a profit.

CHAPTER TWENTY-TWO

Each summer after the 1957 disaster, search parties had gone out from Alpiglen and Eigergletscher and Kleine Scheidegg to canvass the base of the mountains for traces of the two missing Germans, and each year they found everything but the clues they sought. They turned up old ropes, shoes, bits of bivouac gear, a wallet belonging to another dead climber, ice axes and random pitons which had fallen with the rotten rock. A mineral collector found a moldy old climbing jacket, removed the label, and gave it to Stäger, who said it might have come from Nothdurft or Mayer. But beyond this single bit of inconclusive evidence, turned over to the police by Stäger, there were no traces whatsoever of the missing men. Never before in the Eiger's history had bodies remained on the wall for so long, and as each year went by, the mystery grew. Could they have fallen in a crevasse on the upper slopes of the face itself? No, there were no crevasses deep enough to imprison them for four long years; avalanches and rockfalls continually dislodged everything in the gullies of the wall. From experience, the searchers knew that bodies coming down the face fell just to the left or right of the flatiron, the huge spur halfway up, and this limited the search to two relatively small areas at the base. A watch was kept on these spots, but to no avail. Then, in early 1961, four climbers arrived from Munich to undertake the first winter ascent of the north wall. They were led by Toni Hiebeler, editor of *Der Bergkamerad,* the same mountaineering publication which had been taking pot shots at the Swiss ever since the 1957 tragedies. Within a few days, the rope of four had been spotted on the wall; they were proceeding at a slow, steady pace. The weather was cold but clear, and dozens of aircraft came to the valley to take pictures, while an all-Europe television network covered the climb through a long-lens camera at the Kleine Scheidegg hotels.

With the rope now passing through the area where Nothdurft and Mayer had last been seen by Corti, an airplane hired by a Swiss newspaper flew across the wall and a photographer snapped a picture with a wide-angle lens. Back in his darkroom, he printed and enlarged the photograph to see what he had captured. He could make out the two leading Germans high in the exit cracks; he ran his finger down the ropes to a point several hundred feet below, where the other two climbers followed. Off to the right, about fifty or sixty feet from the rope, he spotted what looked like a fifth climber. This was inexplicable; it was well known that there were only four men on the German rope. The photographer took a close look through a magnifying lens, and was certain that he could pick out a fifth human being. The figure was in a vertical position, as indeed it would have to be to remain on the wall. It appeared to be in a funnel-shaped and slightly protected area. No ropes were visible, but the photographer thought he could make out the trousers and upper trunk of a man. The picture was published, and the "fifth man" mystery began to consume the attention of the Oberland. Other photographers chartered planes and took their own pictures, many of them failing to pick up the image because of the outcroppings of rock on either side of the figure. Down at Kleine Scheidegg, in Kaspar von Almen's office, the pictures were blown up and studied through magnifiers and expert opinions were sought. It was pointed out that the "body" was in perfect proportion to the pictures of the four climbers on the wall and that the figure was exactly on the route Nothdurft and Mayer had taken toward the top. To many, there was only one conclusion possible: "the fifth man" was Mayer or Nothdurft, pinned against the wall by his own pitons and ropes in an emergency bivouac established on that Friday night in 1957 when a storm had lashed the face. Others scoffed, among them Seiler and Hiebeler. "I am convinced it is only an outcropping of rock in the shape of a human," Hiebeler said. Seiler made several flights across the face and reported that the "body" was exactly the same gray-blue color as the surrounding rocks. "It looks much less human when seen with binoculars than on photographs," he said. Kaspar von Almen tended to agree, but with no great certainty. "The bodies might have got stuck somewhere, which is not too likely on this almost vertical wall," he said. "But even then we should have found bits and parts of their equipment, pitons or something. No trace was ever found; so there is little doubt they must still be up there, because the theory that they climbed out of the wall via a different route has long been abandoned. The place where the 'body' on the photograph is standing makes sense as a bivouac because it clearly affords some shelter." Nothing could be settled until summer, when search parties might attempt a solution.

But the last-act curtain on the Eiger rescue and its sordid aftermath was fated to fall not on a bold attempt to reconnoiter the face once again but on an accidental scene acted out, with poetic irony, by Werner Stäger and his fellow guides. Toward the end of the 1961 climbing season, during which the eighteenth victim of the north wall had fallen to his death, the guides finally got around to a bit of unfinished business. For two years now, the equipment they had carried to the top of the mountain for the Longhi recovery had remained in place, gradually sinking under the snow and ice of the summit field. No explanation had ever been

provided by the close-mouthed guides; a simple climb up
the west flank would have enabled them to recover the ex-
pensive devices in a matter of hours, just as Friedli and his
crew had brought down their own material a few days
after the rescue of Corti. The guides allowed thousands of
francs worth of gear to remain on the summit.

But in late September, 1961, Stäger organized an action
to salvage the equipment. With several of his fellow guides,
he reached the summit early on a Thursday morning and
found most of the stuff either locked in the ice or damaged
beyond repair. About all that was salvageable was the 1,350
feet of hemp rope which had been purchased from Christian
Rubi. The rope was thick with accumulated moisture and
almost unmanageable; Stäger ordered sections of it wrapped
into bundles and dragged along the mountain. At the west
wall, the men began shoving the bundles downward, catching up and freeing them from obstacles as they became
jammed. One bundle slid along the glacier and fell into a
gully several hundred feet away from the normal west flank
route. The guides climbed down to free it and found two
bodies.

The chance discovery of dead men in the Alps was nothing new to the guides; there were dozens of bodies unac-
counted for in the Oberland. The immediate presumption
was that these were the bodies of two Englishmen who had
last been seen in 1958 while climbing on the Jungfrau
Massif. None of the guides gave a thought to the possibility
that they had happened on the bodies of Nothdurft and
Mayer. Those two must be still on the face, or unaccount-
ably hidden at the base of the north wall. Certainly they
would not be found at this spot to one side of the west flank
ascent route.

Stäger examined the find. The bodies had not been preserved; unlike Longhi's body, they had not been more or

less mummified by the drying winds and the air, but had rotted in their bones until there was only skeleton left. The positions of the remains showed exactly how they had died. One was lying flat on the ground; one was crouched with the back toward the steep wall above. This was the position of men caught in an avalanche, facing away from the thundering ice and snow to avoid suffocation. They had not slipped and fallen; their bones were intact and their clothing was unripped. Their rucksacks were full of metallic equipment, and around their necks were draped necklaces of snap links and pitons. An ice ax hung from the wrist-bones of one body by a small cord. The yellow storm-trousers were perfectly preserved, and the climbing equipment looked almost new. In the rucksack of one, the guides found a blue notebook, but all the writing had been washed away in the rains and melting snows.

The guides marked the bodies and headed down to the rescue station for assistance. They had descended only a short distance when they discovered another body, this one easily identified as Engelberg Titl, a Viennese piano-tuner who had climbed the west wall in 1958 and fallen on the descent. His notebook and climbing gloves had been found at almost exactly the same spot a year before.

The next day a team of guides led by Stäger returned to the mountain and brought the other two bodies down to the inevitable terminal: the mortuary of the Lauterbrunnen cemetery. There close examination indicated that they were the bodies of two Germans. Almost all of their equipment was stamped with the names of German manufacturers. But there were only two Germans missing on the Eiger: Günther Nothdurft and Franz Mayer. A hurried call brought Mayer's sister from her home in Switzerland to the mortuary. She recognized the clothes and the equipment as her brother's, and a final check of the teeth of the dead men provided positive identification. The biggest mystery of the Eiger was solved. Now it was possible to reconstruct the last hours of the two young climbers from Bavaria.

Corti had seen them struggling toward the summit late on the afternoon of Friday, August 9, 1957. Somehow they had gained the top, but probably not before late Friday night, while snow and sleet lashed the north face. The vague report that two climbers had been seen on the summit around midnight Friday—the report which von Almen had relayed to Friedli by radio, and which had been discounted as unreliable—served to show with some precision the length of time, eight or nine hours, it had taken the two Germans to reach the top after leaving Corti. They must, by then, have been almost at the end of their strength. But they had promised to bring help to the two trapped Italians below, and so they began the descent to the Eigergletscher Station five thousand feet down the wind-whipped west flank. It was an act of mercy, conceived in benevolent desperation, but doomed from the beginning. Below them they must have heard the incessant avalanches which Seiler had heard and which had caused the Swiss rescue parties to forego the west wall ascent as too dangerous. Still, the two Germans descended into the objective dangers to find help for their chance ropemates. They had gone only a pathetically short distance down the wall when the avalanche swept them to a suffocating death. As they lay dead under the snow, rescue parties had passed nearby—first Terray and de Booy, then Cassin, Mauri and Eiselin, then the Mountain Guard and the Poles and the rest. But no one had turned to look toward them. Even their tracks had been obliterated by the avalanche.

From the *Totenhalle* of the cemetery, the remains of the two heroic mountaineers—the thirteenth rope ever to climb the north wall—were taken in a hearse to Bavaria. The blue notebook was checked by the criminal investigation division of the Bern police, but it showed nothing. The writing had been washed away, and not even ultraviolet light would bring out the final inscriptions of Günther Nothdurft.

Reporters from *Blick,* a Swiss newspaper, went to Olginate to bring the news to Claudio Corti. As usual, he had no idea of the goings-on at the mountain. With no show of emotion, he said he was happy that his name had been cleared and pleased to hear that others were now writing stories which said, as he had already said so many times himself: "Corti is not a criminal." But he seemed more interested in the fact that his baby daughter had returned that day from the hospital, where she had undergone a successful operation. It was not news to him that he was innocent; let others be surprised. As for his own future, he gave *Blick* a little statement. "I haven't been able to find anybody who is willing to go with me again to the north wall," he said. "But now I'm sure I'll find somebody." Europe shuddered.

EPILOGUE

Where are they all now, and what has happened to their lives?

Seiler and Friedli, hailed in Switzerland as heroes, have gone on to business success in their field: metal fabrication. Seiler owns an automated factory in his native Bönigen, and Friedli has a plant of his own a few miles away. Each benefits from rescue-material contracts with the Swiss Army.

The pressures which brought them at slight loggerheads on the Eiger have long since been forgotten, and each speaks highly of the other. "I cannot tell you how much respect I have for that man Friedli," Seiler says. "I must admit that I did not know his full capacities when we first came together. But I became astonished at his skill, and I will always seek his help when it is needed. I always remember him as he looked on the summit of the Eiger: a strong man, a little older than I, a little bit taller and not so fat, with the face and the manner of a real climber. I think in many ways he was the real hero of the rescue."

Christian Rubi, in his sixties now, has mellowed on every subject except the von Almens, about whom he can still work up a rhetorical sweat. Though partially retired, he leads a busy life as director of the Swiss Ski School Association, and every now and then he turns to the typewriter in his mountainside home in Wengen to take part in one or another of the busy polemics cross-firing over Switzerland. He maintains his position that the 1957 rescue could have been handled more efficiently by professional guides, but he is no longer angry about it. "You see," he says, in a halting but clear English, "it must not be said that I went out of my way to get in a fight with the amateur rescuers. Not at all. It was only when the guides were attacked in the Swiss press that I was forced to come to their defense. Otherwise, I would not have said a word. If you asked me now about the argument and the awful words that were written on both sides, I would say that the whole aftermath was only sad— a sad event that is better forgotten."

The von Almens run their hotels in Kleine Scheidegg and at Trümmelbach in the Lauterbrunnen Valley, and keep up their active interest in the north wall and its climbers. Long years of climbing and studying Alpinism have taught them that none of the clichés about mountaineers are totally true. "I have come to know so many of these men who are willing to attempt the Eiger north wall," Kaspar says, "and I can tell you that they do not only climb it because it is there but for dozens of other complex reasons. Sometimes it is only that they are not getting along at home or because their lives have not been fruitful and they imagine that such a feat would make them famous or respected. Sometimes it is because they are seeking an intense human adventure, a challenge which will enable them to come to grips with themselves. I do not want to judge them as a group. I would make only one general observation. When I hear that a man will be leading a rope on a climb of the sixth degree, I say to myself: 'Well, I wonder what is the matter with him?' "

Nothing seems to be the matter with sixth-degree climber Lionel Terray, whose international reputation both as a climber and rescuer had been firmly established long before *l'affaire* Eiger. He lives in a chalet in Chamonix, the picturesque French village hard against the Mont Blanc Massif. At forty-one, he keeps himself in perfect condition, neither smokes nor drinks, and continues to make climbs on French expeditions all over the world. "I have only three or four more years of sixth-degree climbing left," he says, "and after that I will go to climb the smaller mountains." He has led expeditions to the Himalayas and the Andes since the Eiger rescue. In the wintertime he writes and lectures to raise money for the next summer's activities. His feelings about the Eiger north wall are unchanged. "I would never attempt it again," he says. "The north wall asks too much of a man."

Max Eiselin, the amiable Swiss who threw in his lot with

the rescuers, proved his own high skill on many of the north faces of the Alps after 1957, and capped his exploits by taking part in the first ascent of Dhaulagiri, at 26,811 feet the sixth largest mountain in the world. (With that same Himalayan expedition went Dr. Jerzy Hajdukiewicz, the Pole who had served as a sort of medical officer in the 1957 rescue.) Eiselin is thirty now, a diminutive man with clear hazel eyes, finespun light brown hair and the same friendly manner which endeared him to Terray and his comrades atop the Eiger. He owns a shop—"Eiselin Sport"—in Krienz-Lucerne and specializes in the ironmongery of the elite climbers.

The fires of debate in Lecco have long since been banked, and even Riccardo Cassin has accepted the friendship of Claudio Corti, and gone with him on climbs to the Dolomites. At fifty-three, the pugnacious-appearing Cassin is president of the National Alpine School of Italy and one of the most respected figures in international mountaineering. He is sensitive to the fact that no Italian has ever climbed the north wall (three have died on it), but he is fiercely proud of the record of Italian Alpinists whose exploits include the first ascent of the second largest mountain in the world, the 28,250-foot Mount Godwin Austen (K2) in the Himalayas. "One must be reasonable about the north wall," he says. "I myself have been to its base four times, but conditions have never been right, and I am still alive." In a cluttered little office in the rear of his sports shop in Lecco, Cassin keeps photographs of his famous ropemates of the past and sadly points out how many of them have died in the mountains.

A few kilometers away, Carlo Mauri—that big, amiable man—lives in a villa with his attractive wife and goes off on frequent Italian expeditions all over the world. At thirty-two, his climbing career and his record of ascents continue to flourish. Like American athletes who lend their names to sports products, he serves as an advisor to a factory which produces mountaineering equipment. But he is a wealthy man, and most of his time is spent in the mountains. Like Cassin, he has made his peace with Claudio Corti and occasionally climbs with him in Europe.

Ludwig Gramminger, the merry troll of Munich, is fifty-five now, but his life of service goes on exactly as it has for three decades. He remains the leader of the Munich Mountain Guard, undertakes frequent rescue expeditions, and continues his task of perfecting the machines and devices of his own invention. Almost every army of the free world—including those of the United States, Canada, West Germany, Switzerland and Austria—uses the Gramminger equipment; the royalties go, as they always have, to the Mountain Guard and the German Red Cross. Before any new device is released for use by others, Gramminger takes it into the mountains and tests it, and often he finds himself, despite his advancing years, swinging from the end of a Gramminger cable. "It is only fair," he says, "that I should be the first to test my own equipment."

Like Gramminger, the courageous and powerful Alfred Hellepart is still an active member of the Mountain Guard and remains one of the first persons Gramminger telephones when there is trouble in the mountains. "But I am thirty-six years old now," he says, "and the years have made me a bit overweight and a bit more reasonable; so I no longer make climbs of the sixth degree." An administrative employee of the municipal electrical plant of Munich, he is a nonsmoker, but not, like Terray, for reasons of health. "The reason I do not smoke is the rescue on the Eiger," he says. "You see, men do strange things at high altitude and when they are under extreme tension. When I reached the top with Corti, I asked for a cigarette. Somebody gave me a whole package, and when that was gone, somebody else gave me another package. I was so nervous that I must have smoked thirty cigarettes, and they were the last cigarettes of my life. I made myself sick of them. You might say that this was a small benefit of the rescue, at least for myself."

Another benefit for Hellepart was a lifelong friendship with Claudio Corti. The two correspond frequently in what Hellepart describes as "mutual salutes." When Corti makes a successful climb, he sends Hellepart whole pages bearing on them the words *"Saluti, saluti, saluti. . . ."* And when Hellepart makes a climb, he writes to Corti: "Hellepart sends you many greetings from the mountain." It has become a ritual for the two men who met on a tiny mountain ledge in Switzerland.

On the first anniversary of the rescue, the villagers of Olginate wined and dined Hellepart, gave him medals and speeches and congratulations. "I was very touched," Hellepart says. "Everybody in Olginate must have been there, along with Claudio and his little family. I will tell you— they gave us so much alcohol that I confess I was tipsy after the first hour. The mayor of Olginate gave me a specially struck gold medal; on it was a mountaineer pulling himself up on his icy ax, and there were the words 'Eiger North Wall' and 'Alfred Hellepart.' I treasure this medallion and the friendship of the kind people of Olginate."

And Claudio Corti? What of him?

I interviewed Corti in the spring of 1961, before the German bodies had been found and before his name had been cleared for once and all. It was not without apprehension that my interpreter, Michael Vescoli, and I had driven to the village of Olginate to seek him out. Back in Switzerland, a British newspaperman who covered the 1957 rescue had warned us not to go near Corti. "He is a walking lunatic," the Englishman said. "One never knows what he might do. And he hates journalists." An Italian living in Geneva had told us the same. "It is best that you avoid him," the Italian had said. "He is a crazy man. He still climbs in the mountains around Lecco and Olginate; he waits until he is within sight of a crowd of tourists, and then jumps twenty or thirty feet through the air just to show off. It is even said that once he boarded a train for Spain with the avowed intention of throwing a bomb at Francisco Franco. He is a very wild man, that one!"

Wondering what we would find, and half-expecting the worst, we drove into the dusty village of Olginate on an Italian national holiday to find the streets and alleyways glutted with working people enjoying their extra day off. At a little *trattoria* on the main road, we asked where Corti might be found. "He lives right down the alleyway here," the proprietress told us. "Come, I will take you." She led us along the cobblestones and into a courtyard where a long row of weathered old houses stood. "There," she said, pointing to a door. "That is where that kind man lives."

"Kind man?" we asked.

"Yes," the woman answered. "Everybody in Olginate loves him."

This did not sound like the description of a lunatic. Anxieties allayed, we knocked. Fulvia Losa Corti admitted us and explained that Claudio was off on his motorbike gathering greens for the family rabbits. He would be back soon. Speaking in an elegant, liquid Italian, the handsome woman showed us around the house which had served the Corti family for generations. There was one room for Claudio, Fulvia and their baby, Mariarosa, named after Claudio's late mother; another room for Claudio's father, home at last from his years of migrant work in Switzerland, and a family kitchen. In one corner of the kitchen, there was a big pile of mountaineering gear; in another, a stack of magazines and newspapers—*Il Giorno, Il Tempo, L'Europeo, Paris Match, Der Bund* of Bern and others, all of them full of accounts of the 1957 rescue.

Soon there was a rattling at the door, and in walked Corti, his sleeves rolled up, beads of perspiration on his face. At first glance, he looked too small to be a man who dominated mountains with brute force. But this, like the petulant down-turn of the corners of his mouth, was deceptive. Underneath his plain white shirt, long muscles rippled in his arms, and even his fingers appeared exceptionally strong. They were long and heavy, and of an almost uniform thickness, as big at the tips as they were at the knuckles. One could imagine them probing into the cracks of a steep Alpine face, gripping tightly, and anchoring the weight of his body.

We explained our mission, and were told—in that rapid-fire, mumbling Lombardy dialect—that he would be happy to give us all the time we needed. As he poured *apéritifs,* he made one request: "I would like only that you allow me to tell you the entire story in my own way, and at my own pace."

First, he spoke proudly of Fulvia and the baby. He explained that he still drove the truck for the metal-products factory in Olginate. His salary, for a fifty-hour week, was about twenty dollars. To make ends meet, the family had a small plot of land where they raised vegetables and a few rabbits for meat. He said he considered himself well-off. Like his fellow villagers, he had never known another way of life, and indeed, he fared better than many, with his steady job and the three-room home of his family.

"Now," he announced, "I will take you to my mountains." Thus began a four-hour guided tour of the spires and cliffs of his childhood: the Crigna. Nothing could deter him—not even the broadest hints—from showing us every cliff, every peak, around Lecco and Olginate; then to the mountainside headquarters of the Lecco branch of Club Alpino Italiano, where Corti pointed to photographs of Stefano Longhi on the walls, conducted an inspection of the locker rooms and the storage bins full of ropes and links and pitons, and introduced us to another mountaineer. "Do not forget to write," the other man said in an aside, "that Claudio is the first person to come when there is need to rescue someone. He will never tell you that, but it is true."

"Come," said Corti. "I will show you something else." He asked permission to take the wheel of our car, and began a tire-screeching, Italian-style descent of the twisting road down the mountain. Soon we found ourselves pulling up in front of a cemetery: *San Giovanni Di Lecco*. It was a hot, sunny day, and flowers were everywhere in the graveyard. Many of the tombstones seemed to have been vandalized; there were delicately carved marble arches with two jagged edges where a support had been broken. Said Corti, "They are not that way by accident. When a child is buried here, a part of the tombstone is knocked away deliberately. This is our way of showing that the child's life was broken before it was completed."

In the rear of the cemetery, we came to the grave of Stefano Longhi, still almost new-looking and garnished by flowers. "I come here often," said Corti. "Whenever I climb a mountain, I come here on my motorbike and pay my respects to poor Stefano."

Now it was almost night, and we returned to our hotel in Lecco to hear Corti's account of the rescue on the mountain. For another four hours, he rattled out the details, here and there becoming confused and having to backtrack: "No, it was not Friday. It was Thursday. No, it must have been Friday." He gulped cups of coffee and chain-smoked the harsh, green-packaged Nazionali cigarettes. His attitude, on the whole, was that of a man who had undergone experiences which he had not yet been able to assimilate or comprehend. Years of defending himself had made him intense and defensive. Over and over he repeated how hard he and Stefano had trained, how well prepared they had

been for the Eiger, how it was only the accidents of Nothdurft's illness and Stefano's slip and the falling rock which
had brought the climb to a tragic end. "Imagine," he said,
"they keep saying that Stefano was not qualified, that he
was too old and not in condition. And yet he was able to
endure nine nights on that wall, more than any other man
in history. Does that sound like the record of a man who
was not in condition?"

There was no stopping him as he mumbled on, repeating
himself, defending himself and even more strongly defending Longhi. "Stefano was a good man and a strong climber,"
he said. "That is why I positioned him at the end of the
rope, because his strength would have been needed if the
sick German had slipped."

It was late at night when the three of us got in the car
for the short drive from Lecco back to Corti's home in
Olginate. He was still expressing dismay—never anger—
at the attacks on him and reiterating his rationalizations.
Finally, he talked about his own attitude toward the Eiger.
"I do not like that place," he said, "and I will have it or it
will have me. It is only that Fulvia is afraid, and that I am
having trouble finding someone to go with me. That mountain hurt me; it hurt my hands and it hurt my head and it
cost me eighteen of my teeth, and most of all it took Stefano.
I tell you: I dream about it all the time, that evil wall in the
Oberland. I never dream of my climb with Stefano, or my
rescue; I dream that I am on the summit and I have climbed
the wall, and I am at peace. I must go back."

So we had found not a lunatic, not a braggart or a liar,
and certainly not a criminal, but only a driven, befuddled
child in the body of a man. We remembered the words of
Carlo Mauri: "To me, it always seemed that Claudio was
a child on the mountains, a child possessed of great natural
ability and tremendous strength, but nevertheless a child
trying to show his father he is not afraid." And Kaspar von

Almen: "When I hear that a man will be leading a rope on a climb of the sixth degree, I say to myself: 'Well, I wonder what is the matter with him?' "

We had found a naïve and simple man who had made the mountains his mode of existence, his only true reality, the place where he worked off all the frustrations and humiliations that bedevil the lives of the poor. In another society, he might have become a drinker or a compulsive maker of ship models or a chaser of butterflies. But all he had known was the mountains and the single-minded need to reach their tops, and reach their tops again, as though in defeating them he were defeating all the forces of evil, the goblins and demons and ogres that fill the thoughts of the very young. If other men died alongside him, it was sad, but it did not change matters. The issue was only more sharply joined with each death. One could sense no theme of apologia in his visits to Stefano Longhi's grave, but rather a feeling that he was visiting the little cemetery merely to commune with a comrade-in-arms who had once fought the battle at his side, and to promise that there would be no surrender, that the wall which had beaten them back would be attacked again and again in much the same way that a child, hot with anger, remounts the tricycle which has thrown him down.

And now it would seem that the life of Claudio Corti must lead, with blunt singularity of purpose, back to the instrument of his defeat. "I will have it or it will have me." Worse men exist. We are all children, but we are not all brave.

ABOUT THE AUTHOR

JACK OLSEN is the author of twenty-seven books published in fifteen countries and in eleven languages. A former bureau chief for *Time,* he has written for *Vanity Fair*, *Life*, *People*, and *Reader's Digest*. He has won citations for excellence from Columbia and Indiana Universities, three Edgar Award nominations, and the 1990 Edgar for *Doc: The Rape of the Town of Lovell*. He lives on an island in Washington's Puget Sound.